By Katsuaki Togo
with Fujiko Motohashi

Pocket Japanese

Quick Access to Everyday Phrases ▷ ▷ ▷

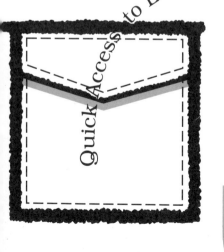

PJ

This book is based on *Swift and Sure English Conversation*, by Katsuaki Togo, published by The Japan Times. All the commentaries were written specially for this book by Fujiko Motohashi.

First edition: November 1993
12th printing: June 2002

Jacket design: Aurora DeAurora

Published by The Japan Times, Ltd.
5-4, Shibaura 4-chome, Minato-ku, Tokyo 108-0023, Japan
Phone: 03-3453-2013
http://bookclub.japantimes.co.jp/

ISBN4-7890-0716-2

Printed in Japan

Preface

A Japanese Conversation Survival Kit——

I am a teacher of English and a linguist by profession. I was, and still am, a learner of English, too. People often ask me how I learnt to speak English. I always reply that I learned it the hard way. But this would not probably satisfy them, because they expect me to give more practical suggestions. So I usually recommended one of my books entitled *Swift and Sure English Conversation*.

Since its first publication more than hundreds of thousands of English learners in almost all walks of life in Japan have used it and found it of great help and use. It provides essential expressions needed for daily conversation. Moreover, thanks to its unique format you can look them up whenever you need them. Since it turned out to be very handy and useful, there has been great demand for the same edition in languages other than English. It has been published for the purpose of teaching conversation in more than fifteen different languages. I do not see why we should not produce its Japanese version.

With the help of Ms. Motohashi, an expert in Japanese language teaching, it has been carefully rewritten. It is strongly recommended to anyone who is keen on learning daily colloquial Japanese.

This will certainly serve as a survival kit for ensuring your daily communication with the local people. As an old saying goes, "When in Rome, do as the Romans do," ——when in Japan, speak as the Japanese speak.

I wish you the best of luck!

Katsuaki Togo

Contents

Part 1 ○ **Everyday Phrases**

Part 2 ● Expressions in Conversation

About This Book

This book consists of two parts.

Part 1 provides you with phrases that will use in everyday situations: greetings, basic questions, expressions related to time and date, the accepting and turning down of invitations, etc. These phrases appear quite frequently in daily conversation. Use them to communicate in natural Japanese.

Part 2 is the main part of this book. Here you will find more than 60 basic sentence patterns that are usually learned in the early stages of Japanese language study. There are a number of helpful example sentences listed under each pattern.

Suppose you want to apologize. You can quickly access the right expression by looking up "I'm sorry" in the phrase index (Index 1) or else "Apologizing" in the situation index (Index 2). Both indices are at the back of the book.

You will also find a glossary at the back. Not only does this serve as a handy English-Japanese dictionary, but it is also cross-referenced, so you can use it to help you find the Japanese phrase you want.

After you find the phrase you need, take a look at the other sentences on the page. This way, you'll get a general idea of how the sentence pattern is used, what situations it's used in, and what functions it has.

And don't stop with just reading the examples. Try making up other sentences on your own, sentences that fit your own specific needs. This kind of practice will no doubt help you come up with the right phrase when you're speaking Japanese in real situations.

Many of the sections contain a brief commentary. This will give you important information on how and when to use the expressions——and when *not* to. These commentaries will also teach you other useful expressions that are used in the given situation.

Please carry this book around with you: Both a survival tool and a handy study guide, it will greatly improve your Japanese communication skills.

Part 1

Everyday Phrases

1 Greetings

☐ Good morning. ▶ おはようございます。
Ohayoo-gozaimasu.

☐ Good afternoon./ ▶ こんにちは。
Hello. Konnichiwa.

☐ Good evening. ▶ こんばんは。
Konbanwa.

☐ Good night. ▶ おやすみなさい。
Oyasuminasai.

☐ Goodbye. ▶ さようなら。
Sayoonara.

On seeing someone in the morning, you can use the greeting **Ohayoo-gozaimasu** no matter who the other person is—a family member, a co-worker, your boss, etc. With, however, **Konnichiwa**, which is used in the afternoon, and **Konbanwa**, which is used from the evening on, you have to be a little careful. With such people as family members and co-workers you see on a daily business—in other words, people who are in your "in group"—you do not use these greetings; if you use them with these people you will sound a little strange and distant. So if, in the afternoon, you happen to run into a co-worker somewhere outside the company, say, **Aa, xx-san, doomo**; when you return to your office during the day, say **Tadaima**.

As for **Sayoonara**, do not use this with a superior. **Shitsuree-shimasu** is more appropriate. ■

2 Meeting someone for the first time

☐ My name is Kimura.

▶（私は）木村と申します。
(Watashi-wa) Kimura-to moo-shi-masu.

☐ This is Mr. Johnson.

▶こちらは ジョンソンさんです。
Kochira-wa Jonson-san-desu.

☐ A: How do you do?

▶A: はじめまして、どうぞ よろしく（お願いします）。
Hajimemashite, doozo yoro-shiku (onegai-shimasu).

B: How do you do?

B: こちらこそ どうぞ よろしく（お願いします）。
Kochira-koso doozo yoro-shiku (onegai-shimasu).

After saying *Hajimemashite* you give your name. For adults it's customary to say just your last name. Remember that in Japan there is no custom of shaking hands while introducing oneself in this way. The usual practice is to bow your head slightly while saying *Hajimemashite*. At first this may be rather difficult, but with practice you will find yourself getting used to it.

People frequently identify themselves further with the help of the particle *no*. One way is to give the name of your company, as in *Japan-Taimuzu-no Tanaka-desu* (Tanaka of The Japan Times). Another is to state your position, as in *Kenshuusee-no Sumisu-desu* (Smith, a research student). Businessmen will exchange name cards as they introduce themselves in this way. ∎

3 When you don't understand

□ I beg your pardon.
▶ すみませんが, もう一度
言ってください。
Sumimasen-ga, moo ichido itte-kudasai.

□ Please speak a little more slowly.
▶ すみませんが, もう すこし
ゆっくり 話してください。
Sumimasen-ga, moo sukoshi yukkuri hanashite-kudasai.

□ I'm sorry. I don't understand.
▶ すみませんが, よく わかり
ません。
Sumimasen-ga, yoku wakari-masen.

□ I understand now.
▶ よく わかりました。
Yoku wakarimashita.

Whether it's the price, a telephone number, or a difficult name, there will be times when you just can't catch what was said. In these cases, these expressions are nothing less than basic survival tools. But what happens when even after someone has repeated it slowly, you still don't understand? The best thing is to ask that the information be written: *Sumimasen, kaite-kudasai* (Excuse me, could you write it please?) or else *Sumimasen, Roomaji-de kaite-kudasai* (Excuse me, write it in Roman characters please). Such phrases as *Eego-ga wakaru kata imasu-ka* (Is there someone here who speaks English?) or else *Sumimasen, Nihongo-ga yoku wakarimasen* (Excuse me, I don't speak Japanese well) may also come in handy. ■

4 Talking about the weather

☐ Nice day, isn't it?
▶ いい お天気ですね。
Ii otenki-desu-ne.

☐ Hot today, isn't it?
▶ 暑いですね。
Atsui-desu-ne.

☐ Cold, isn't it?
▶ 寒いですね。
Samui-desu-ne.

☐ Bad weather, isn't it?
▶ いやな お天気ですね。
Iya-na otenki-desu-ne.

☐ Muggy, isn't it?
▶ むし暑いですね。
Mushiatsui-desu-ne.

☐ It's been raining a lot, hasn't it?
▶ よく 降りますね。
Yoku furimasu-ne.

After exchanging greetings such as *Ohayoo-gozaimasu*, we often talk just for a little bit about the weather. Especially when we're passing the time with someone we don't know very well, it's a convenient topic of conversation: The fine weather, the temperature—these are things that everyone has in common.

Because there are four distinct seasons in Japan, there is no lack of climate-related topics. For example, when the seasons are changing, you'll often hear *Suzushiku/atatakaku narimashita-nee* (It's gotten cool/warm, hasn't it?). Another phrase you'll often hear in Japan is *Yatto tsuyu-ga akemashita-nee* (The rainy season has finally ended). ■

5 Expressing gratitude

□ Thank you very much. ▶ ありがとうございます。
Arigatoo-gozaimasu.

□ Thank you very much for your kindness. ▶ いろいろ ありがとうございました。
Iroiro arigatoo-gozaimashita.

□ Thank you for the pleasant evening. ▶ ごちそうさまでした。
Gochisoosama-deshita.

□ A: Thank you for inviting me. ▶ A: お招きいただいて ありがとうございます。
Omaneki-itadaite arigatoo-gozaimasu.

B: You're welcome. B: どういたしまして。
Doo itashimashite.

□ I'm glad I could help you. ▶ お役に 立てて 幸せです。
Oyaku-ni tatete shiawase-desu.

□ Any time. ▶ いつでも どうぞ。
Itsu-demo doozo.

□ A: Thank you for all your help. ▶ A: いろいろ お世話に なりました。
Iroiro osewa-ni narimashita.

B: Don't mention it. B: とんでもありません。
Tondemo-arimasen.

6 Apologizing

☐ I'm sorry.
▶ どうも すみません。
Doomo sumimasen.

☐ Please forgive me.
▶ どうか お許しください。
Dooka oyurushi-kudasai.

☐ I'm awfully sorry.
▶ 本当に 申し訳ございません。
Hontoo-ni mooshiwake-gozaimasen.

☐ I'm sorry.
▶ 失礼いたしました。
Shitsuree-itashimashita.

☐ Excuse me.
▶ 失礼。
Shitsuree.

☐ That's all right.
▶ どう いたしまして。
Doo itashimashite.

☐ No, that's my fault.
▶ 私の 方こそ すみません。
Watakushi-no hoo-koso sumimasen.

In the course of daily life there are many situations where we have to apologize—for example, in a rush-hour train, when we step on someone's foot or our baggage knocks into someone. In these cases it's best to say promptly, **A, doomo sumimasen** (Oh, excuse me). If you're late for meeting someone, say **Osoku-natte sumimasen** (I'm sorry I'm late) or else **Renraku-dekinakute sumimasen** (I'm sorry I couldn't get in touch with you). You can use the ~**te** form of a verb to describe the offense for which you are apologizing. With close friends **Gomennasai** (Pardon me) is used. Remember that in Japan it is considered proper to acknowledge one's mistakes and apologize. ■

☐ Excuse me, but . . .　　▶ちょっと おうかがいしま
　　　　　　　　　　　　すが……。
　　　　　　　　　　　Chotto oukagai-shimasu-ga . . .

☐ Excuse me, but . . .　　▶失礼ですが……。
　　　　　　　　　しつれい
　　　　　　　　　　　Shitsuree-desu-ga . . .

☐ Pardon me, but . . .　　▶すみませんが……。
　　　　　　　　　　　Sumimasen-ga . . .

☐ Say . . .　　　　　　　▶あのう……。
　　　　　　　　　　　Anoo . . .

When we're walking along the street somewhere, we will never approach someone and suddenly say, for example, *Chikatetsu-no iriguchi-wa doko-desu-ka* (Where is the entrance to the subway station?). Without fail we will preface our question with one of the phrases above. If we don't, we will seem abrupt and rude.

When we want to ask a question to a superior or a teacher, we must realize that we're asking them to spare some of their time for us, so it's best to say first something like *Anoo, ima chotto yoroshii-deshoo-ka* (May I bother you for a moment now?) or *Sumimasen, shitsumon-ga aru-n-desu-ga* (Excuse me, but I have a question...). You could say these phrases open the doors to conversations. ■

(8) Conversational responses

☐ Is that right?
▶ ああ，そうですか。
Aa, soo-desu-ka.

☐ I see.
▶ なるほど。
Naruhodo.

☐ Really?
▶ 本当ですか。
Hontoo-desu-ka.

☐ I didn't know that.
▶ それは知りませんでした。
Sore-wa shirimasen-deshita.

☐ Yes?
▶ それで。
Sore-de.

☐ I know what you mean.
▶ そうですね。
Soo-desu-ne.

☐ Unbelievable.
▶ 信じられません。
Shinjiraremasen.

☐ How fortunate!
▶ よかったですね。
Yoketta-desu-ne.

☐ Yes. (*Indicates that one understands what is being said*.)
▶ ええ。
Ee.

☐ Yes. (*Indicates that one understands what is being said*.)
▶ はい。
Hai.

These phrases, called *aizuchi*, are a fundamental part of Japanese conversation. They are used by the listening party to encourage the speaker to continue. They are interspersed in the pauses in the speaker's words. Please note that *Ee* and *Hai* do not necessarily indicate agreement with what the speaker is saying; they simply indicate that the listener is following the flow of thought. ■

⑨ Expressing sympathy

☐ That's too bad. ▶ それは いけませんね。
Sore-wa ikemasen-ne.

☐ That's too bad. ▶ それは こまりましたね。
Sore-wa komarimashita-ne.

☐ That's terrible. ▶ それは ひどいですね。
Sore-wa hidoi-desu-ne.

☐ I'm sorry to hear that. ▶ それは 残念ですね。
Sore-wa zannen-desu-ne.

☐ I know how you feel. ▶ お気持ちは よく わかります。
Okimochi-wa yoku wakarimasu.

☐ May I offer my deepest condolences? ▶ 心から おくやみ 申し上げます。
Kokoro-kara okuyami mooshi-agemasu.

It's difficult to express sympathy in a fitting way: We worry both about saying something that might unintentionally upset the person we're trying to console, and also about saying some stiff set-phrase that does not have any warmth. But we should remember that when someone's sad or depressed, very often there's no real need to say very much. In those cases it's probably best simply to say the phrases above in a soft voice. To someone who is deeply grieving the loss of a family member, you might start off with a phrase like *Hontoo-ni nanto ittara ii-ka...* (I really don't know what to say). ∎

(10) Expressing agreement

☐ That's right.
▶ 全く その通りです。
Mattaku sono toori-desu.

☐ I think so, too.
▶ 私も そう 思います。
Watashi-mo soo omoimasu.

☐ I quite agree.
▶ 全く 同感です。
Mattaku dookan-desu.

☐ I also agree with that.
▶ それは 私も 賛成です。
Sore-wa watashi-mo sansee-de-su.

In addition to *Watashi-mo soo omoimasu* (I think so too), *Hontoo-ni soo-desu-nee* (That really is true, isn't it?) is another of many ways to express agreement. *Sono toori* (It's just as you say), *dookan* (I agree), and *sansee* (I agree) are also often used to express agreement during an exchange of opinions. A note of caution, however: If you use these words when talking with a superior, you'll come off sounding somewhat pompous, since these words imply that the listener is judging the ideas of the speaker.

Even more difficult than expressing agreement is expressing disagreement. This is because Japanese tend to avoid directly contradicting others. When you want to disagree, you can say something like *Watashi-no iken-wa sukoshi chigau-n-desu-ga...* (My opinion is just a little bit different, though...). It's best, though, to preface this with a hesitant phrase, such as *Soo-desu-ka(↘), uun...* (Is that so?...well...). This will help soften your disagreement. ■

- [ ] Please remember me to your family. ▶おうちの 皆さんに よろしく お伝えください。
Ouchi-no minasan-ni yoroshiku otsutae-kudasai.

- [ ] Please give my regards to your wife. ▶奥様に よろしく お伝えください。
Okusama-ni yoroshiku otsutae-kudasai.

- [ ] Please give my regards to your husband. ▶ご主人様に よろしく お伝えください。
Goshujinsama-ni yoroshiku otsutae-kudasai.

- [ ] Please give my regards to Mr. Brown. ▶ブラウンさんに よろしく お伝えください。
Buraun-san-ni yoroshiku otsutae-kudasai.

- [ ] Please say hello to Mary for me. ▶メアリーに よろしく。
Mearii-ni yoroshiku.

Otsutae-kudasai is a polite form for tsutaete-kudasai (Please give my message). When someone asks you Yoroshiku otsutae-kudasai (Please give my regards [to someone]), you should reply Hai, tsutaemasu (Yes, I will) or Wakarimashita (Yes, I will). When asked to give regards to your family, first say Arigatoo-gozaimasu (Thank you).

When you actually pass along regards from someone, you should say, Nakamura-san-ga yoroshiku-to itte-imashita (Nakamura-san says hello). In place of itte-imashita, you can use the honorific osshatte-imashita. ■

12 Time

☐ What time is it? ▶ 今 何時ですか。
Ima nanji-desu-ka.

☐ It's just five. ▶ ちょうど 5時です。
Choodo goji-desu.

☐ It's a quarter past five. ▶ 5時15分すぎです。
Goji juugofun-sugi-desu.

☐ It's half past five. ▶ 5時半です。
Goji-han-desu.

☐ It's five minutes to six. ▶ 6時5分前です。
Rokuji gofun-mae-desu.

☐ I'm sorry, but I don't ▶ すみません。時計を 持って
have a watch. いませんので。
Sumimasen. Tokee-o motte-
imasen-node.

Although there will be occasions when you don't have to be all that precise about the time, you'll find that in Japan it is important to be able to discuss time in exact, to-the-minute terms. Trains almost always run exactly on time, and events and meetings will also open at precisely the scheduled time. Thus when you hear the patterns ～wa ～ji-kara-desu/made-desu (It starts from ～ o'clock/It lasts until ～ o'clock), assume that the times given are the precise times. You will find the following kinds of phrases helpful: *Tsugi-no densha-wa nanji-desu-ka* (What time is the next train?); *Kaigi-wa nanji-kara-desu-ka* (What time does the meeting start?); *Eega-wa nanji-made-desu-ka* (What time does the movie end?).

Note also *rokuji-goro* (around 6 o'clock), *gozen rokuji* (6 a.m.), and *gogo rokuji* (6 p.m.). ■

13 Length of time

☐ How long will it take? ▶ どのぐらい かかりますか。
Dono-gurai kakarimasu-ka.

☐ Ten minutes. ▶ 10分です。
Juppun-desu.

☐ Thirty minutes. ▶ 30分 です。
Sanjuppun-desu.

☐ An hour. ▶ 1時間です。
Ichijikan-desu.

☐ Two-and-a-half hours. ▶ 2時間半です。
Nijikan-han-desu.

☐ Half a day. ▶ 半日です。
Hannichi-desu.

☐ Three days. ▶ 3日です。
Mikka-desu.

☐ Three weeks. ▶ 3週間です。
Sanshuukan-desu.

☐ One month. ▶ 1か月です。
Ikkagetsu-desu.

☐ Two-and-a-half months. ▶ 2か月半です。
Nikagetsu-han-desu.

☐ Half a year. ▶ 半年です。
Hantoshi-desu.

☐ One year. ▶ 1年です。
Ichinen-desu.

☐ Two-and-a-half years. ▶ 2年半です。
Ninen-han-desu.

14 The days of the week

□ What day is March 1 ? ▶ 3月1日は 何曜日ですか。
がつついたち なにようび
Sangatsu tsuitachi-wa naniyoo-bi-desu-ka.

□ It's Monday. ▶ 月曜日です。
げつようび
Getsuyoobi-desu.

□ It's Tuesday. ▶ 火曜日です。
かようび
Kayoobi-desu.

□ It's Wednesday. ▶ 水曜日です。
すいようび
Suiyoobi-desu.

□ It's Thursday. ▶ 木曜日です。
もくようび
Mokuyoobi-desu.

□ It's Friday. ▶ 金曜日です。
きんようび
Kin'yoobi-desu.

□ It's Saturday. ▶ 土曜日です。
どようび
Doyoobi-desu.

□ It's Sunday. ▶ 日曜日です。
にちようび
Nichiyoobi-desu.

When we talk about the days of the week we often use abbreviated forms—for example: *Getsu, sui, kin-wa kaigi-ga arimasu* (There are meetings on Monday, Wednesday, and Friday); *Doo, nichi-wa uchi-ni imasu* (I'm at home on Saturdays and Sundays/I'll be at home on Saturday and Sunday); *Kaa, moku-wa jikan-ga arimasu* (I have time on Tuesday and Thursday).

In any given month a certain day of the week will come around four or five times. You can specify, for example, precisely which Saturday, by saying *dai-ichi/dai-ni/dai-san/dai-yon/dai-go doyoobi* (the first/second/third/fourth/fifth Saturday of the month).

15 Dates

☐ When is your birth-day?

▶ 誕生日は 何月何日ですか。
Tanjoobi-wa nangatsu nan-nichi-desu-ka.

☐ It's January 1.

▶ 1月1日です。
Ichigatsu tsuitachi-desu.

☐ It's February 2.

▶ 2月2日です。
Nigatsu futsuka-desu.

☐ It's March 3.

▶ 3月3日です。
Sangatsu mikka-desu.

☐ It's April 4.

▶ 4月4日です。
Shigatsu yokka-desu.

☐ It's May 5.

▶ 5月5日です。
Gogatsu itsuka-desu.

☐ It's June 6.

▶ 6月6日です。
Rokugatsu Muika-desu.

☐ It's July 7.

▶ 7月7日です。
Shichigatsu nanoka-desu.

☐ It's August 8.

▶ 8月8日です。
Hachigatsu yooka-desu.

☐ It's September 9.

▶ 9月9日です。
Kugatsu kokonoka-desu.

☐ It's October 10.

▶ 10月10日です。
Juugatsu tooka-desu.

☐ It's November 14.

▶ 11月 14日です。
Juuichigatsu juuyokka-desu.

☐ It's December 20.

▶ 12月20日です。
Juunigatsu hatsuka-desu.

☐ It's December 24.

▶ 12月 24日 です。
Juunigatsu nijuuyokka-desu.

16 Saying which day

☐ When is/was that? ▶ それは いつですか。
Sore-wa itsu-desu-ka.

☐ It was the day before yesterday. ▶ おとといです。
Ototoi-desu.

☐ It was yesterday. ▶ きのうです。
Kinoo-desu.

☐ It's today. ▶ きょうです。
Kyoo-desu.

☐ It's tomorrow. ▶ あしたです。
Ashita-desu.

☐ It's the day after tomorrow. ▶ あさってです。
Asatte-desu.

☐ It was ten days ago. ▶ 10日前です。
Tooka-mae-desu.

☐ It was last Tuesday. ▶ 先週の 火曜日です。
Senshuu-no kayoobi-desu.

☐ It's this Friday. ▶ 今週の 金曜日です。
Konshuu-no kin'yoobi-desu.

☐ It's next Monday. ▶ 来週の 月曜日です。
Raishuu-no getsuyoobi-desu.

☐ It's next Sunday. ▶ 今度の 日曜日です。
Kondo-no nichiyoobi-desu.

☐ It was this past Saturday. ▶ この 前の 土曜日です。
Kono mae-no doyoobi-desu.

☐ It's the end of this month. ▶ 今月の 末です。
Kongetsu-no sue-desu.

☐ It's the middle of next month. ▶ 来月の 中ごろです。
Raigetsu-no naka-goro-desu.

☐ It's next year. ▶ 来年です。
Rainen-desu.

17 Asking the price

☐ How much is it (are they)? ▶ いくらですか。
Ikura-desu-ka.

☐ How much is it all together? ▶ 全部で いくらですか。
Zenbu-de ikura-desu-ka.

☐ Are service charges included? ▶ サービス料は 入っています か。
Saabisuryoo-wa haitte-imasu-ka.

☐ How much is it duty-free? ▶ 免税で いくらですか。
Menzee-de ikura-desu-ka.

☐ Is there tax on this? ▶ 消費税が かかりますか。
Shoohizee-ga kakarimasu-ka.

Whether or not a purchase fits your budget certainly is an important matter. For this reason, it would be a good idea to remember these phrases: *Koohii/hako-dai/sooryoo-wa betsu-ryookin-desu-ka* (Is coffee/the box/postage extra?); *Nani-ka betsuni hiyoo-ga kakarimasu-ka* (Will there be any additional expenses?); *Moo sukoshi yasui monowa arimasen-ka* (Isn't there something a little less expensive?).

If there's some figure on the receipt that you don't understand, ask *Sumimasen, kore-wa nan-no kingaku-desu-ka* (Excuse me, what is this figure for?). ■

18 Expressing likes and dislikes

☐ I really like it (them). ▶ これは すきです。
Kore-wa suki-desu.

☐ I don't really like this (these) very much. ▶ これは あまり すきじゃ ありません。
Kore-wa amari suki-ja arima-sen.

☐ I love this food. ▶ これは 大好物です。
Kore-wa daikoobutsu-desu.

☐ I'm not very fond of this food. ▶ これは 苦手なんです。
Kore-wa nigate-na-n-desu.

If, for example, you're talking about how even when you were a child you didn't like milk, you can use such blunt expressions as *Miruku-wa kirai-desu* (I don't like milk).

When you've been invited to dinner, however, it's a different matter. This of course is because the food that's in front of you is something that your host has kindly provided. If you find that you've been served something you can't eat, say, *Sumi-masen, ika-wa taberaremasen* (I'm sorry, I can't eat squid); *Kore-wa chotto nigate-na-n-desu* (I'm afraid I don't really like this); *Osake-wa dame-na-n-desu* (I don't drink). These phrases should keep you from hurting your host's feelings—as long, of course, as you gobble up the other dishes! ■

19 Expressing emotions

☐ I'm so happy. ▶ うれしいです。
Ureshii-desu.

☐ I'm enjoying myself. ▶ 楽しいです。
Tanoshii-desu.

☐ I'm so sad. ▶ 悲しいです。
Kanashii-desu.

☐ I'm lonely. ▶ さびしいです。
Sabishii-desu.

☐ I'm so sorry. ▶ 残念です。
Zannen-desu.

☐ I'm disappointed. ▶ がっかりしました。
Gakkari-shimashita.

☐ I'm very worried. ▶ 心配です。
Shinpai-desu.

☐ I feel very uneasy. ▶ 不安です。
Fuan-desu.

☐ I'm afraid. ▶ こわいです。
Kowai-desu.

☐ I was surprised. ▶ びっくりしました。
Bikkuri-shimashita.

☐ I was shocked. ▶ おどろきました。
Odorokimashita.

☐ This is interesting. ▶ おもしろいです。
Omoshiroi-desu.

☐ This is boring. ▶ つまらないです。
Tsumaranai-desu.

20 Talking about one's health

☐ I'm tired. ▶ 疲れました。
Tsukaremashita.

☐ I'm sleepy. ▶ ねむいです。
Nemui-desu.

☐ I have a headache. ▶ 頭が 痛いです。
Atama-ga itai-desu.

☐ I have a stomachache. ▶ 胃が 痛いです。
I-ga itai-desu.

☐ I have a toothache. ▶ 歯が 痛いです。
Ha-ga itai-desu.

☐ I have a cold. ▶ カゼです。
Kaze-desu.

☐ I have diarrhea. ▶ 下痢です。
Geri-desu.

☐ I have a temperature. ▶ 熱が あります。
Netsu-ga arimasu.

☐ My stomach hurts. ▶ おなかが 痛いです。
Onaka-ga itai-desu.

☐ I feel dizzy. ▶ めまいが します。
Memai-ga shimasu.

☐ My chest hurts. ▶ 胸が くるしいです。
Mune-ga kurushii-desu.

☐ I'm constipated. ▶ 便秘です。
Benpi-desu.

□ Hello, is that the Thomas' residence?
▶もしもし，トーマスさんのお宅ですか。
Moshi-moshi, Toomasu-san-no otaku-desu-ka.

□ This is Mr. Thomas.
▶はい，トーマスですが。
Hai, Toomasu-desu-ga.

□ Who's calling, please?
▶どちらさまですか。
Dochirasama-desu-ka.

□ May I speak to Mr. Kitamura, please?
▶北村さん お願いします。
Kitamura-san onegai-shimasu.

□ Just a moment, please.
▶少々 お待ちください。
Shooshoo omachi-kudasai.

□ Mr. Kitamura, there's a phone call for you.
▶北村さん，お電話ですよ。
Kitamura-san, odenwa-desu-yo.

□ Will you answer the phone?
▶ちょっと 出てください。
Chotto dete-kudasai.

□ Please phone me again at 10.
▶10時に もう 一度 お電話ください。
Juuji-ni moo ichido odenwa-kudasai.

□ I'll call back later.
▶あとで また お電話します。
Ato-de mata odenwa-shimasu.

□ Goodbye.
▶ごめんください。
Gomen-kudasai.

□ You have the wrong number.
▶ちがいます。
Chigaimasu.

22 Accepting invitations

☐ I'd be glad to. ▶ ええ よろこんで。
Ee, yorokonde.

☐ I'll definitely be there. ▶ ぜひ うかがいます。
Zehi ukagaimasu.

☐ I'd be glad to join you. ▶ お供させていただきます。
Otomo-sasete-itadakimasu.

☐ I'd be glad to come. ▶ お邪魔させていただきます。
Ojama-sasete-itadakimasu.

How you respond to an invitation depends on just what you're being invited to. If someone says *Chotto biiru-demo nomimasen-ka* (Shall we go have a beer?), you can reply *Ii-desu-nee, ikima-shoo* (That sounds good. Let's go).

If someone says, *Raishuu uchi-ni shokuji-ni irasshaimasen-ka* (Would you like to come over for dinner next week?), first show a little reserve, asking *Ii-n-desu-ka* (May I?). After that you accept, saying *Yorokonde ukagaimasu* (I'd love to). If someone says *Raishuu issho-ni (o)hanami-ni ikimasen-ka* (Would you like to go cherry-blossom-viewing next week?), you can answer *Aa, ii-desu-nee, hanami-wa hajimete-na-n-desu. Zehi goissho-shimasu* (Oh, that would be nice. I've never been cherry-blossom-viewing before. Yes, I'd love to go with you).

If you're invited to a party or a celebration, it's customary upon arriving at the event to say something like *Kyoo-wa goshootai arigatoo-gozai-mashita* (Thank you very much for inviting me). ■

(23) Turning down invitations

- [ ] I'm sorry, but I won't be able to come.

▶ 残念ですが……。
Zannen-desu-ga . . .

- [ ] Let's make it some other time.

▶ 次の 機会に ぜひ お願いします。
Tsugi-no kikai-ni zehi onegai-shimasu.

- [ ] I have a previous engagement.

▶ すみませんが, 先約が ありますので……。
Sumimasen-ga, sen'yaku-ga arimasu-node . . .

- [ ] I can't make it today.

▶ 今日は ちょっと……。
Kyoo-wa chotto . . .

When people invite you to join them for something, they'll often use such lines as *Konshuu-no doyoobi-wa nani-ka yotee-ga arimasu-ka* (Do you have any plans for this Saturday?), *Raishuu-no nichiyoobi-wa hima-desu-ka* (Are you free next Sunday?). If you want to turn down such an invitation, please avoid such direct responses as *Ikemasen* (I can't go) or *Ikitaku-arimasen* (I don't want to go). You should, to begin with, use an expression that shows you feel bad about having to turn down the kind invitation. Thus you should first say *Doyoobi desu-ka* (Saturday?) in a somewhat troubled manner, to indicate that there is a conflict. Then say *Sekkaku-desu-ga, doyoobi-wa chotto dame-na-n-desu* (Thank you, but I'm afraid I can't on Saturday). It will also help to remember this line: *Mata sasotte-kudasai* (Please invite me some other time). ■

(24) Entertaining

☐ Please come in.　　　　　▶どうぞ お入りください。
　　　　　　　　　　　　　　　Doozo ohairi-kudasai.

☐ This way, please.　　　　▶こちらへ どうぞ。
　　　　　　　　　　　　　　　Kochira-e doozo.

☐ Please sit down.　　　　　▶どうぞ おかけください。
　　　　　　　　　　　　　　　Doozo okake-kudasai.

☐ Just a moment.　　　　　▶しばらく お待ちください。
　　　　　　　　　　　　　　　Shibaraku omachi-kudasai.

☐ Please make yourself　　▶お楽に なさってください。
　 at home.　　　　　　　　　Oraku-ni nasatte-kudasai.

☐ Do you like it (them)?　　▶これは おすきですか。
　　　　　　　　　　　　　　　Kore-wa osuki-desu-ka.

☐ Please help yourself.　　▶どうぞ 召し上がってくだ
　　　　　　　　　　　　　　　さい。
　　　　　　　　　　　　　　　Doozo meshiagatte-kudasai.

☐ Please relax and enjoy　▶今日は ゆっくり なさって
　 yourself.　　　　　　　　　ください。
　　　　　　　　　　　　　　　Kyoo-wa yukkuri nasatte-kuda-
　　　　　　　　　　　　　　　sai.

As you can see, the phrases above will be used by
the person who is inviting someone else in. Of
course it's also important to know the phrases used
by the person being invited in: On entering someone's house, say *Ojama-shimasu*; on leaving, put it
in the past tense: *Ojama-shimashita*. On entering a
place like an office, say *Shitsuree-shimasu*; on
leaving, you can either repeat *Shitsuree-shimasu* or
else put it in the past: *Shitsuree-shimashita.* ■

㉕ Excusing oneself

□ I must go now.

▶ それでは そろそろ 失礼い
たします。
Sore-dewa sorosoro shitsuree-itashimasu.

□ I have to get up early tomorrow, so I must go now.

▶ あしたの 朝 早いので, この 辺で 失礼します。
Ashita-no asa hayai-node, kono hen-de shitsuree-shimasu.

□ I must go now.

▶ もう 行かなくては なりませんので……。
Moo ikanakute-wa narimasen-node...

□ Goodbye. (*Said when leaving before others.*)

▶ すみませんが, お先に 失礼 します。
Sumimasen-ga, osaki-ni shitsu-ree-shimasu.

Before you excuse yourself with such expressions as *Sayoonara* or *Shitsuree-shimasu*, you should indicate your intention to leave. If during a pleasant gathering you suddenly stand up and say *Kaerimasu* (I'm leaving) or *Kaeranakereba narimasen* (I have to go), you may spoil the mood of the party.

Although it's a little old-fashioned, the phrase *Sore-dewa sorosoro oitoma-shimasu* (I have to be going) is still often used. Some other expressions that will come in handy when you want to leave are *A, moo kuji-desu-ne, sukkari ojama-shimashi-ta/sukkari gochisoo-ni narimashita* (Why, it's 9 o'clock already. Thank you so much [literally, I've been such a bother]/It was a delicious meal). ■

Part 2

Expressions in Conversation

1 Thank you

☐ Thank you for your letter.

☐ Thank you for calling me.

☐ Thank you for your reply.

☐ Thank you for inviting me.

☐ Thank you for the other day.

☐ Thank you for taking the trouble to come out here.

☐ Thank you for helping me.

☐ Thank you for teaching me.

Japanese are taught from childhood the importance of gratitude. And many people consider **Arigatoo** to be their favorite word.

In the examples above **Arigatoo-gozaimashita** is in the past tense. There are times, however, when you want to show that you are feeling gratitude right now—for example, when someone picks up and hands you something that you dropped on the street. In those cases, say **Arigatoo-gozaimasu**. ↗

ありがとう Arigatoo

▶ お手紙 ありがとうございました。
  Otegami arigatoo-gozaimashita.

▶ お電話 ありがとうございました。
  Odenwa arigatoo-gozaimashita.

▶ お返事 ありがとうございました。
  Ohenji arigatoo-gozaimashita.

▶ ご招待 ありがとうございました。
  Goshootai arigatoo-gozaimashita.

▶ 先日は ありがとうございました。
  Senjitsu-wa arigatoo-gozaimashita.

▶ わざわざ おいでいただいて ありがとうございました。
  Wazawaza oide-itadaite arigatoo-gozaimashita.

▶ お手伝いいただいて ありがとうございました。
  Otetsudai-itadaite arigatoo-gozaimashita.

▶ 教えていただいて ありがとうございました。
  Oshiete-itadaite arigatoo-gozaimashita.

When served coffee at someone's house, some people will say *Arigatoo-gozaimasu* and some will say **Sumimasen**. Both phrases express gratitude. Some foreigners, however, may wonder why Japanese, in order to show gratitude, apologize. The reason for this is the feeling that they have made someone take the trouble to do something for their sake.

■

2 Is there a ~?

☐ Is there a hotel near here?

☐ Is there a parking lot near here?

☐ Is there a bank near here?

☐ Is there a post office near here?

☐ Is there a department store near here?

☐ Is there a police station near here?

☐ Is there a drugstore near here?

☐ Is there a bus stop near here?

☐ Is there a train station near here?

☐ Is there a hospital near here?

☐ Is there a restaurant near here?

☐ Is there a supermarket near here?

☐ Is there a movie theater near here?

☐ Is there a public telephone near here?

☐ Is there a rest room near here?

☐ Is there a cloakroom near here?

☐ Is there an information desk near here?

ありますか (1) Arimasu-ka

▶ この辺に ホテル ありますか。
Kono-hen-ni hoteru arimasu-ka.

▶ この辺に 駐車場 ありますか。
Kono-hen-ni chuushajoo arimasu-ka.

▶ この辺に 銀行 ありますか。
Kono-hen-ni ginkoo arimasu-ka.

▶ この辺に 郵便局 ありますか。
Kono-hen-ni yuubinkyoku arimasu-ka.

▶ この辺に デパート ありますか。
Kono-hen-ni depaato arimasu-ka.

▶ この辺に 交番 ありますか。
Kono-hen-ni kooban arimasu-ka.

▶ この辺に 薬局 ありますか。
Kono-hen-ni yakkyoku arimasu-ka.

▶ この辺に バス停 ありますか。
Kono-hen-ni basutee arimasu-ka.

▶ この辺に 電車の 駅 ありますか。
Kono-hen-ni densha-no eki arimasu-ka.

▶ この辺に 病院 ありますか。
Kono-hen-ni byooin arimasu-ka.

▶ この辺に レストラン ありますか。
Kono-hen-ni resutoran arimasu-ka.

▶ この辺に スーパーマーケット ありますか。
Kono-hen-ni suupaamaaketto arimasu-ka.

▶ この辺に 映画館 ありますか。
Kono-hen-ni eegakan arimasu-ka.

▶ この辺に 公衆電話 ありますか。
Kono-hen-ni kooshuudenwa arimasu-ka.

▶ この辺に トイレ ありますか。
Kono-hen-ni toire arimasu-ka.

▶ この辺に クローク ありますか。
Kono-hen-ni kurooku arimasu-ka.

▶ この辺に 案内所 ありますか。
Kono-hen-ni annaijo arimasu-ka.

3 Do you have ~?

- ☐ Do you have film?

- ☐ Do you have toothpaste?

- ☐ Do you have soap?

- ☐ Do you have cigarettes?

- ☐ Do you have stamps?

- ☐ Do you have post cards?

- ☐ Do you have envelopes?

- ☐ Do you have writing paper?

- ☐ Do you have maps?

- ☐ Do you have a telephone directory?

- ☐ Do you have this?

- ☐ Do you have this in other colors?

- ☐ Do you have bread?

- ☐ Do you have coffee?

- ☐ Do you have sandwiches?

- ☐ Do you have juice?

- ☐ Do you have beer?

ありますか ② Arimasu-ka

▶ フィルム ありますか。
Fuirumu arimasu-ka.

▶ 歯みがき ありますか。
Hamigaki arimasu-ka.

▶ 石けん ありますか。
Sekken arimasu-ka.

▶ たばこ ありますか。
Tabako arimasu-ka.

▶ 切手 ありますか。
Kitte arimasu-ka.

▶ はがき ありますか。
Hagaki arimasu-ka.

▶ 封筒 ありますか。
Fuutoo arimasu-ka.

▶ 便せん ありますか。
Binsen arimasu-ka.

▶ 地図 ありますか。
Chizu arimasu-ka.

▶ 電話帳 ありますか。
Denwachoo arimasu-ka.

▶ これと 同じもの ありますか。
Kore-to onaji mono arimasu-ka.

▶ ほかの 色 ありますか。
Hoka-no iro arimasu-ka.

▶ パン ありますか。
Pan arimasu-ka.

▶ コーヒー ありますか。
Koohii arimasu-ka.

▶ サンドイッチ ありますか。
Sandoitchi arimasu-ka.

▶ ジュース ありますか。
Juusu arimasu-ka.

▶ ビール ありますか。
Biiru arimasu-ka.

Do you have ~?／Can I go by~?

Questions one might be asked ·····················

☐ Do you have an I.D. card?

☐ Do you have a passport?

☐ Do you have a visa?

☐ Do you have your credit card?

☐ Do you have the receipt?

☐ Do you have any luggage?

☐ Do you have anything to declare?

☐ Do you have any money?

Asking about transportation ·······················

☐ Can I go there by bus?

☐ Can I go there by train?

☐ Can I go there by subway?

☐ Can I make the last train?

When making a reservation ·······················

☐ Do you have any seats?

☐ Do you have any rooms?

☐ Do you have any tables?

ありますか ③ Arimasu-ka

▶ 身分証明書は ありますか。
Mibunshoomeesho-wa arimasu-ka.

▶ パスポートは ありますか。
Pasupooto-wa arimasu-ka.

▶ ビザは ありますか。
Biza-wa arimasu-ka.

▶ クレジットカードは ありますか。
Kurejittokaado-wa arimasu-ka.

▶ 領収書は ありますか。
Ryooshuusho-wa arimasu-ka.

▶ 荷物は ありますか。
Nimotsu-wa arimasu-ka.

▶ 課税品は ありますか。
Kazeehin-wa arimasu-ka.

▶ お金は ありますか。
Okane-wa arimasu-ka.

▶ そこまで バスは ありますか。
Soko-made basu-wa arimasu-ka.

▶ そこまで 電車は ありますか。
Soko-made densha-wa arimasu-ka.

▶ そこまで 地下鉄は ありますか。
Soko-made chikatetsu-wa arimasu-ka.

▶ 終電は まだ ありますか。
Shuuden-wa mada arimasu-ka.

▶ 席は ありますか。
Seki-wa arimasu-ka.

▶ 部屋は ありますか。
Heya-wa arimasu-ka.

▶ テーブルは ありますか。
Teeburu-wa arimasu-ka.

5 How about ～? (1)

Offering refreshments ······························

☐ How about a cup of coffee?

☐ How about a cup of tea?

☐ How about a cup of green tea?

☐ How about a cigarette?

☐ How about some beer?

☐ How about some sake?

☐ How about some wine?

☐ How about some whiskey?

☐ How about some juice?

☐ How about some fruit?

☐ How about some sandwiches?

☐ How about some ice cream?

Inviting someone out ···························

☐ How about going to a movie?

☐ How about going out for dinner?

☐ How about going to the party?

☐ How about going to the concert?

いかがですか (1) Ikaga-desu-ka

▶ コーヒー(は) いかがですか。
Koohii(-wa) ikaga-desu-ka.

▶ 紅茶(は) いかがですか。
Koocha(-wa) ikaga-desu-ka.

▶ 日本茶(は) いかがですか。
Nihoncha(-wa) ikaga-desu-ka.

▶ たばこ(は) いかがですか。
Tabako(-wa) ikaga-desu-ka.

▶ ビール(は) いかがですか。
Biiru(-wa) ikaga-desu-ka.

▶ 日本酒(は) いかがですか。
Nihonshu(-wa) ikaga-desu-ka.

▶ ワイン(は) いかがですか。
Wain(-wa) ikaga-desu-ka.

▶ ウィスキー(は) いかがですか。
Uisukii(-wa) ikaga-desu-ka.

▶ ジュース(は) いかがですか。
Juusu(-wa) ikaga-desu-ka.

▶ くだもの(は) いかがですか。
Kudamono(-wa) ikaga-desu-ka.

▶ サンドイッチ(は) いかがですか。
Sandoitchi(-wa) ikaga-desu-ka.

▶ アイスクリーム(は) いかがですか。
Aisukuriimu(-wa) ikaga-desu-ka.

▶ 映画 いっしょに いかがですか。
Eega issho-ni ikaga-desu-ka.

▶ 食事 いっしょに いかがですか。
Shokuji issho-ni ikaga-desu-ka.

▶ パーティー いっしょに いかがですか。
Paatii issho-ni ikaga-desu-ka.

▶ コンサート いっしょに いかがですか。
Konsaato issho-ni ikaga-desu-ka.

6 How about ～? (2)

Suggesting means of transportation ·············

☐ How about going by subway?

☐ How about taking a taxi?

☐ How about taking a bus?

☐ How about flying?

☐ How about walking?

Suggesting a time ·····························

☐ How about tomorrow?

☐ How about next week?

☐ How about next month?

☐ How about next Monday?

☐ How about this afternoon?

☐ How about tomorrow morning?

Suggesting a place ····························

☐ How about in my office?

☐ How about in my house?

☐ How about at the hotel lobby?

☐ How about at the same place as last time?

いかがですか ② Ikaga-desu-ka

▶ 地下鉄で 行ったら いかがですか。
Chikatetsu-de ittara ikaga-desu-ka.

▶ タクシーで 行ったら いかがですか。
Takushii-de ittara ikaga-desu-ka.

▶ バスで 行ったら いかがですか。
Basu-de ittara ikaga-desu-ka.

▶ 飛行機で 行ったら いかがですか。
Hikooki-de ittara ikaga-desu-ka.

▶ 歩いたら いかがですか。
Aruitara ikaga-desu-ka.

▶ あしたは いかがですか。
Ashita-wa ikaga-desu-ka.

▶ 来週は いかがですか。
Raishuu-wa ikaga-desu-ka.

▶ 来月は いかがですか。
Raigetsu-wa ikaga-desu-ka.

▶ 今度の 月曜日は いかがですか。
Kondo-no getsuyoobi-wa ikaga-desu-ka.

▶ きょうの 午後は いかがですか。
Kyoo-no gogo-wa ikaga-desu-ka.

▶ あしたの 午前中は いかがですか。
Ashita-no gozenchuu-wa ikaga-desu-ka.

▶ 私の 会社では いかがですか。
Watashi-no kaisha-dewa ikaga-desu-ka.

▶ 私の うちでは いかがですか。
Watashi-no uchi-dewa ikaga-desu-ka.

▶ ホテルの ロビーでは いかがですか。
Hoteru-no robii-dewa ikaga-desu-ka.

▶ この 間の 場所では いかがですか。
Kono aida-no basho-dewa ikaga-desu-ka.

7 I want to go ～.

- ☐ I want to go by car.

- ☐ I want to go by taxi.

- ☐ I want to go by train.

- ☐ I want to go by express train.

- ☐ I want to go by limited express.

- ☐ I want to go by bus.

- ☐ I want to go by subway.

- ☐ I want to walk.

- ☐ I want to go by bicycle.

- ☐ I want to go by motorbike.

- ☐ I want to go by ship.

- ☐ I want to go by plane.

- ☐ I want to go alone.

- ☐ I want to go later.

- ☐ I want to go only with you.

- ☐ I want to go with my family.

- ☐ I want to go with my children.

(〜で) 行きたい (〜de) Ikitai

▶ 車 で 行きたいんですが。
Kuruma-de ikitai-n-desu-ga.

▶ タクシーで 行きたいんですが。
Takushii-de ikitai-n-desu-ga.

▶ 電車で 行きたいんですが。
Densha-de ikitai-n-desu-ga.

▶ 急行で 行きたいんですが。
Kyuukoo-de ikitai-n-desu-ga.

▶ 特急で 行きたいんですが。
Tokkyuu-de ikitai-n-desu-ga.

▶ バスで 行きたいんですが。
Basu-de ikitai-n-desu-ga.

▶ 地下鉄で 行きたいんですが。
Chikatetsu-de ikitai-n-desu-ga.

▶ 歩いて 行きたいんですが。
Aruite ikitai-n-desu-ga.

▶ 自転車で 行きたいんですが。
Jitensha-de ikitai-n-desu-ga.

▶ オートバイで 行きたいんですが。
Ootobai-de ikitai-n-desu-ga.

▶ 船で 行きたいんですが。
Fune-de ikitai-n-desu-ga.

▶ 飛行機で 行きたいんですが。
Hikooki-de ikitai-n-desu-ga.

▶ 一人で 行きたいんですが。
Hitori-de ikitai-n-desu-ga.

▶ あとで 行きたいんですが。
Ato-de ikitai-n-desu-ga.

▶ 二人きりで 行きたいんですが。
Futarikiri-de ikitai-n-desu-ga.

▶ 家族で 行きたいんですが。
Kazoku-de ikitai-n-desu-ga.

▶ 子供連れで 行きたいんですが。
Kodomozure-de ikitai-n-desu-ga.

8 I want to go to ～ (go ～ing).

Destinations ••

☐ I want to go to the airport.

☐ I want to go to this hotel.

☐ I want to go to the embassy.

☐ I want to go to the bank.

☐ I want to go to the the post office.

☐ I want to go to this restaurant.

☐ I want to go to the hospital.

☐ I want to go to the police station.

☐ I want to go to this movie theater.

Pastimes ••

☐ I want to go swimming.

☐ I want to go driving.

☐ I want to go skiing.

☐ I want to go on a picnic.

☐ I want to go fishing.

☐ I want to go bowling.

☐ I want to go shopping.

(〜に)行きたい (〜ni) Ikitai

▶ 空港に 行きたいんですが。
Kuukoo-ni ikitai-n-desu-ga.

▶ この ホテルに 行きたいんですが。
Kono hoteru-ni ikitai-n-desu-ga.

▶ 大使館に 行きたいんですが。
Taishikan-ni ikitai-n-desu-ga.

▶ 銀行に 行きたいんですが。
Ginkoo-ni ikitai-n-desu-ga.

▶ 郵便局に 行きたいんですが。
Yuubinkyoku-ni ikitai-n-desu-ga.

▶ この レストランに 行きたいんですが。
Kono resutoran-ni ikitai-n-desu-ga.

▶ 病院に 行きたいんですが。
Byooin-ni ikitai-n-desu-ga.

▶ 交番に 行きたいんですが。
Kooban-ni ikitai-n-desu-ga.

▶ この 映画館に 行きたいんですが。
Kono eegakan-ni ikitai-n-desu-ga.

▶ 泳ぎに 行きたいです。
Oyogi-ni ikitai-desu.

▶ ドライブに 行きたいです。
Doraibu-ni ikitai-desu.

▶ スキーに 行きたいです。
Sukii-ni ikitai-desu.

▶ ピクニックに 行きたいです。
Pikunikku-ni ikitai-desu.

▶ 釣りに 行きたいです。
Tsuri-ni ikitai-desu.

▶ ボーリングに 行きたいです。
Booringu-ni ikitai-desu.

▶ 買い物に 行きたいです。
Kaimono-ni ikitai-desu.

9 Is that (Am I on) the right ~?

☐ Is that the right bus to Shinjuku? / Am I on the right bus to Shinjuku?

☐ Is that the right train to Osaka? / Am I on the right train to Osaka?

☐ Is that the right subway to Ikebukuro? / Am I on the right subway to Ikebukuro?

☐ Is that the right ship to Kawasaki? / Am I on the right ship to Kawasaki?

These phrases can be used both when you are riding a train and when you are on the platform. An important one to remember is **Kono densha-wa doko-iki-desu-ka** (Where does this train go?).

At big stations where many lines stop, even Japanese will get confused if they are not familiar with the place. Here are some more phrases that should help you when you're not sure which train or bus to take.

Chuuoo-sen-wa nan-bansen-desu-ka. (What track is the Chuo Line?)

〜行きですか 〜Iki desu-ka

▶ この バスは 新宿行きですか。
Kono basu-wa Shinjuku-iki-desu-ka.

▶ この 電車は 大阪行きですか。
Kono densha-wa Oosaka-iki-desu-ka.

▶ この 地下鉄は 池袋行きですか。
Kono chikatetsu-wa Ikebukuro-iki-desu-ka.

▶ この 船は 川崎行きですか。
Kono fune-wa Kawasaki-iki-desu-ka.

Odakyuu-sen-wa kono hoomu-desu-ka/koko-desu-ka. (Is this the platform for the Odakyu Line?)

Shinjuku-iki-no basu-wa nan-ban-desu-ka. (What's the number of the bus that goes to Shinjuku?)

Kono densha-wa tokkyuu/kyuukoo/kakueki-desu-ka. (Is this train a limited express/an express/a local?)

Kono densha-wa Yotsuya-ni tomarimasu-ka. (Does this train stop at Yotsuya?)

■

10 How much ~? (1)

Prices in a store ·······················

☐ How much is this?

☐ How much is that?

☐ How much will that be altogether?

☐ How much is it duty-free?

☐ How much is it including consumption tax?

Prices in a hotel ·······················

☐ What's the charge for a single room?

☐ What's the charge for a double room?

☐ What's the charge for a twin room?

☐ How much is the service charge?

☐ How much is the tax?

Prices at the post office ·······················

☐ How much is the postage for this?

☐ How much is a post card?

☐ How much is it by air mail?

☐ How much is it by sea mail?

☐ How much is it by special delivery?

いくらですか (1) Ikura-desu-ka

- ▶ これは いくらですか。
  Kore-wa ikura-desu-ka.

- ▶ あれは いくらですか。
  Are-wa ikura-desu-ka.

- ▶ 全部で いくらですか。
  Zenbu-de ikura-desu-ka.

- ▶ 免税で いくらですか。
  Menzee-de ikura-desu-ka.

- ▶ 消費税込みで いくらですか。
  Shoohizee-komi-de ikura-desu-ka.

- ▶ シングルは いくらですか。
  Shinguru-wa ikura-desu-ka.

- ▶ ダブルは いくらですか。
  Daburu-wa ikura-desu-ka.

- ▶ ツインは いくらですか。
  Tsuin-wa ikura-desu-ka.

- ▶ サービス料は いくらですか。
  Saabisuryoo-wa ikura-desu-ka.

- ▶ 税金は いくらですか。
  Zeekin-wa ikura-desu-ka.

- ▶ これは いくらですか。
  Kore-wa ikura-desu-ka.

- ▶ はがきは いくらですか。
  Hagaki-wa ikura-desu-ka.

- ▶ 航空便で いくらですか。
  Kookuubin-de ikura-desu-ka.

- ▶ 船便で いくらですか。
  Funabin-de ikura-desu-ka.

- ▶ 速達で いくらですか。
  Sokutatsu-de ikura-desu-ka.

11 How much ～? (2)

Asking about fares ·····························

☐ How much is the fare?

☐ How much is a one-way ticket to Kyoto?

☐ How much is a round-trip ticket to Kyoto?

☐ How much is a first-class ticket to Kyoto?

☐ How much is the limited express to Nagano?

☐ How much is a one-way ticket to Tokyo for a child?

☐ How much is a ride? (*at an amusement park*)

☐ How much is the taxi fare to the airport?

Miscellaneous ·····························

☐ Check, please./Bill, please.

☐ What is the admission fee?

☐ How much is a haircut?

☐ How much is a set and shampoo?

☐ How much is the rent?

☐ How much is the consumption tax?

いくらですか ⑵ Ikura-desu-ka

▶ 運賃は いくらですか。
Unchin-wa ikura-desu-ka.

▶ 京都まで 片道 いくらですか。
Kyooto-made katamichi ikura-desu-ka.

▶ 京都まで 往復 いくらですか。
Kyooto-made oofuku ikura-desu-ka.

▶ 京都まで グリーン車で いくらですか。
Kyooto-made guriinsha-de ikura-desu-ka.

▶ 長野まで 特急で いくらですか。
Nagano-made tokkyuu-de ikura-desu-ka.

▶ 東京まで 子供 片道 いくらですか。
Tookyoo-made kodomo katamichi ikura-desu-ka.

▶ 乗り物 1回 いくらですか。
Norimono ikkai ikura-desu-ka.

▶ 空港まで タクシーで いくらぐらいですか。
Kuukoo-made takushii-de ikura-gurai-desu-ka.

▶ おいくらですか。
Oikura-desu-ka.

▶ 入場料は いくらですか。
Nyuujooryoo-wa ikura-desu-ka.

▶ カットは いくらですか。
Katto-wa ikura-desu-ka.

▶ セットと シャンプーで いくらですか。
Setto-to shanpuu-de ikura-desu-ka.

▶ 家賃は いくらですか。
Yachin-wa ikura-desu-ka.

▶ 消費税は いくらですか。
Shoohizee-wa ikura-desu-ka.

12 When ～?

- [ ] When is your birthday?

- [ ] When will you have your wedding?

- [ ] When will you take the examination?

- [ ] When will you have a party?

- [ ] When is your payday?

- [ ] When are you leaving?

- [ ] When will you be back?

- [ ] When is the deadline?

- [ ] When does the vacation begin?

- [ ] When were you born?

- [ ] When did you enter the school?

- [ ] When did you graduate? /When are you going to graduate?

- [ ] When did you join the company?

- [ ] When did you come to Japan?

- [ ] When are you going back to your country?

いつですか Itsu-desu-ka

▶ お誕生日は いつですか。
Otanjoobi-wa itsu-desu-ka.

▶ ご結婚式は いつですか。
Gokekkonshiki-wa itsu-desu-ka.

▶ 試験は いつですか。
Shiken-wa itsu-desu-ka.

▶ パーティーは いつですか。
Paatii-wa itsu-desu-ka.

▶ 給料日は いつですか。
Kyuuryoobi-wa itsu-desu-ka.

▶ ご出発は いつですか。
Goshuppatsu-wa itsu-desu-ka.

▶ お帰りは いつですか。
Okaeri-wa itsu-desu-ka.

▶ 締め切りは いつですか。
Shimekiri-wa itsu-desu-ka.

▶ 休暇は いつですか。
Kyuuka-wa itsu-desu-ka.

▶ お生まれは いつですか。
Oumare-wa itsu-desu-ka.

▶ 入学は いつですか。
Nyuugaku-wa itsu-desu-ka.

▶ 卒業は いつですか。
Sotsugyoo-wa itsu-desu-ka.

▶ 入社は いつですか。
Nyuusha-wa itsu-desu-ka.

▶ 来日は いつですか。
Rainichi-wa itsu-desu-ka.

▶ ご帰国は いつですか。
Gokikoku-wa itsu-desu-ka.

13 Would you ~?/I'd like to ~.

On the phone ···

☐ I'd like extention 212.

☐ I'd like the front desk.

☐ I'd like room service.

☐ I'd like Mr. Hayashi of the public relations department.

☐ I'd like the number for the Japan Times.

☐ I'd like to make a collect call.

At the post office ···

☐ Would you take care of this?

☐ Would you send this by sea mail?

☐ Would you send this by air mail?

☐ Would you send this by registered mail?

☐ Would you send this by special delivery?

At the hotel ···

☐ Would you call a taxi for me?

☐ I'd like to pay the bill.

☐ I'd like to check out.

お願いします Onegai-shimasu

▶ 内線 212 お願いします。
Naisen ni-ichi-ni onegai-shimasu.

▶ フロント お願いします。
Furonto onegai-shimasu.

▶ ルームサービス お願いします。
Ruumusaabisu onegai-shimasu.

▶ 広報部の 林さんを お願いします。
Koohoobu-no Hayashi-san-o onegai-shimasu.

▶ ジャパンタイムズ社の 電話番号 お願いします。
Japantaimuzu-sha-no denwabangoo onegai-shimasu.

▶ コレクトコールで お願いします。
Korekutokooru-de onegai-shimasu.

▶ (郵便物を) お願いします。
(Yuubinbutsu-o) onegai-shimasu.

▶ 船便で お願いします。
Funabin-de onegai-shimasu.

▶ 航空便で お願いします。
Kookuubin-de onegai-shimasu.

▶ 書留で お願いします。
Kakitome-de onegai-shimasu.

▶ 速達で お願いします。
Sokutatsu-de onegai-shimasu.

▶ タクシー お願いします。
Takushii onegai-shimasu.

▶ お勘定 お願いします。
Okanjoo onegai-shimasu.

▶ チェックアウト お願いします。
Chekkuauto onegai-shimasu.

14 Congratulations!

- [ ] Happy New Year!

- [ ] Happy New Year!

- [ ] Happy birthday to you!

- [ ] Congratulations on your marriage!

- [ ] Congratulations on your passing the exam (for entrance to a school, a license, etc.)!

- [ ] Congratulations on your victory!

- [ ] Congratulations on having a baby!

- [ ] Congratulations on your recovery!

- [ ] Congratulations on your 50th anniversary!

- [ ] Congratulations on the completion of the new building!

- [ ] Congratulations on your acceptance at the school!

- [ ] Congratulations on your promotion!

- [ ] Congratulations on your promotion!

- [ ] Congratulations on your graduation!

- [ ] Congratulations on your new job!

- [ ] Congratulations on winning the prize!

おめでとう Omedetoo

▶ あけまして おめでとうございます。
Akemashite omedetoo-gozaimasu.

▶ 新年 おめでとうございます。
Shinnen omedetoo-gozaimasu.

▶ お誕生日 おめでとうございます。
Otanjoobi omedetoo-gozaimasu.

▶ ご結婚 おめでとうございます。
Gokekkon omedetoo-gozaimasu.

▶ 合格 おめでとうございます。
Gookaku omedetoo-gomaimasu.

▶ 優勝 おめでとうございます。
Yuushoo omedetoo-gozaimasu.

▶ ご出産 おめでとうございます。
Goshussan omedetoo-gozaimasu.

▶ ご全快 おめでとうございます。
Gozenkai omedetoo-gozaimasu.

▶ 50周年記念 おめでとうございます。
Gojusshuunen-kinen omedetoo-gozaimasu.

▶ 完成記念 おめでとうございます。
Kansee-kinen omedetoo-gozaimasu.

▶ ご入学 おめでとうございます。
Gonyuugaku omedetoo-gozaimasu.

▶ ご栄転 おめでとうございます。
Goeeten omedetoo-gozaimasu.

▶ ご昇格 おめでとうございます。
Goshookaku omedetoo-gozaimasu.

▶ ご卒業 おめでとうございます。
Gosotsugyoo omedetoo-gozaimasu.

▶ ご就職 おめでとうございます。
Goshuushoku omedetoo-gozaimasu.

▶ 入賞 おめでとうございます。
Nyuushoo omedetoo-gozaimasu.

15 I'll get off ~.

☐ I'll get off here.

☐ I'll get off at the next stop.

☐ I'll get off at the second stop.

☐ I'll get off at the end of the line.

☐ I'll get off at the third stop.

☐ I'll get off at the fourth stop.

☐ I'll get off at the fifth stop.

☐ I'll get off at Shinjuku.

☐ I'll get off at the next signal.

☐ I'll get off at the crossing.

The phrases above can be used when you're asked **Doko-de orimasu-ka** (Where will you get off?). Another situation in which you'll have to indicate where you will get off is when you're in a taxi. Note that then you can use the transitive form of **oriru**—**orosu**—as in **Ekimae-de oroshite-kudasai** (Please let me off in front of the station).

If you're on a sightseeing bus and you want ↗

おります Orimasu

▶ ここで おります。
Koko-de orimasu.

▶ 次で おります。
Tsugi-de orimasu.

▶ 次の 次で おります。
Tsugi-no tsugi-de orimasu.

▶ 終点で おります。
Shuuten-de orimasu.

▶ 3つ目で おります。
Mittsu-me-de orimasu.

▶ 4つ目で おります。
Yottsu-me-de orimasu.

▶ 5つ目で おります。
Itsutsu-me-de orimasu.

▶ 新宿で おります。
Shinjuku-de orimasu.

▶ 次の 信号で おります。
Tsugi-no shingoo-de orimasu.

▶ その 交差点で おります。
Sono koosaten-de orimasu.

↘to go, say, to a lake, you can ask the bus driver *Mizuumi-ni ikitai-n-desu-ga, doko-de orireba ii-desu-ka* (I'd like to go to the lake. Where should I get off?). He'll give a reply like *Kohan-guchi-de orite-kudasai. Orite-kara juugofun-gurai aruki-masu-yo* (Get off at Kohan-guchi. It's about a fifteen-minute walk from there).

■

16   I have (a) ~./I feel ~.

Describing symptoms ·····························

- [ ] I have a headache.

- [ ] I feel sick.

- [ ] I have a chill.

- [ ] I have a stomachache.

- [ ] I feel out of breath.

- [ ] I have a ringing in my ears.

- [ ] I feel dizzy.

- [ ] I have heartburn.

Describing sensations ·····························

- [ ] I hear a strange noise.

- [ ] Something smells good.

- [ ] It tastes sweet.

〜がします　~Ga shimasu

▶頭痛が します。
Zutsuu-ga shimasu.

▶吐き気が します。
Hakike-ga shimasu.

▶寒気が します。
Samuke-ga shimasu.

▶腹痛が します。
Fukutsuu-ga shimasu.

▶息切れが します。
Ikigire-ga shimasu.

▶耳鳴りが します。
Miminari-ga shimasu.

▶目まいが します。
Memai-ga shimasu.

▶胸やけが します。
Muneyake-ga shimasu.

▶変な 音が します。
Henna oto-ga shimasu.

▶いい におい がします。
Ii nioi-ga shimasu.

▶甘い 味が します。
Amai aji-ga shimasu.

17 I don't like ～. (1)

Food ··

☐ I don't like rice.

☐ I don't like fish.

☐ I don't like eggs.

☐ I don't like meat.

☐ I don't like sashimi.

☐ I don't like octopus.

☐ I don't like natto.

☐ I don't like umeboshi.

☐ I don't like takuan.

☐ I don't like sweets.

Drinks ··

☐ I don't like beer.

☐ I don't like whiskey.

☐ I don't like Coke.

☐ I don't like sake.

☐ I don't like green tea.

☐ I don't like coffee.

▶お米は きらいです。
Okome-wa kirai-desu.

▶魚は きらいです。
Sakana-wa kirai-desu.

▶卵は きらいです。
Tamago-wa kirai-desu.

▶肉は きらいです。
Niku-wa kirai-desu.

▶さしみは きらいです。
Sashimi-wa kirai-desu.

▶タコは きらいです。
Tako-wa kirai-desu.

▶納豆は きらいです。
Nattoo-wa kirai-desu.

▶うめぼしは きらいです。
Umeboshi-wa kirai-desu.

▶たくあんは きらいです。
Takuan-wa kirai-desu.

▶甘い 物は きらいです。
Amai mono-wa kirai-desu.

▶ビールは きらいです。
Biiru-wa kirai-desu.

▶ウィスキーは きらいです。
Uisukii-wa kirai-desu.

▶コーラは きらいです。
Koora-wa kirai-desu.

▶日本酒は きらいです。
Nihonshu-wa kirai-desu.

▶日本茶は きらいです。
Nihoncha-wa kirai-desu.

▶コーヒーは きらいです。
Koohii-wa kirai-desu.

61

18 I don't like ～. (2)

Pastimes ･･････････････････････････････････････

- ☐ I don't like reading books.

- ☐ I don't like karaoke.

- ☐ I don't like noisy music.

- ☐ I don't like TV.

- ☐ I don't like cooking.

- ☐ I don't like traveling.

- ☐ I don't like sports.

- ☐ I don't like bowling.

- ☐ I don't like playing golf.

- ☐ I don't like skiing.

- ☐ I don't like skating.

- ☐ I don't like fishing.

- ☐ I don't like dancing.

- ☐ I don't like playing mahjong.

- ☐ I don't like playing cards.

きらいです ② Kirai-desu

▶ 読書は きらいです。
Dokusho-wa kirai-desu.

▶ カラオケは きらいです。
Karaoke-wa kirai-desu.

▶ うるさい 音楽は きらいです。
Urusai ongaku-wa kirai-desu.

▶ テレビは きらいです。
Terebi-wa kirai-desu.

▶ 料理は きらいです。
Ryoori-wa kirai-desu.

▶ 旅行は きらいです。
Ryokoo-wa kirai-desu.

▶ スポーツは きらいです。
Supootsu-wa kirai-desu.

▶ ボーリングは きらいです。
Booringu-wa kirai-desu.

▶ ゴルフは きらいです。
Gorufu-wa kirai-desu.

▶ スキーは きらいです。
Sukii-wa kirai-desu.

▶ スケートは きらいです。
Sukeeto-wa kirai-desu.

▶ 釣りは きらいです。
Tsuri-wa kirai-desu.

▶ ダンスは きらいです。
Dansu-wa kirai-desu.

▶ 麻雀は きらいです。
Maajan-wa kirai-desu.

▶ トランプは きらいです。
Toranpu-wa kirai-desu.

Purchases ··

☐ A one-way to Niigata, please.

☐ A one-way for a child to Niigata, please.

☐ A round-trip to Nagano, please.

☐ A round-trip for a child to Nagano, please.

☐ Ten 41-yen stamps, please.

☐ Seven post cards, please.

☐ A 36 exposure roll for color prints, please.

☐ A toothbrush, please.

☐ Some toothpaste, please.

☐ A pack of cigarettes, please.

☐ Half a dozen bottles of beer, please.

☐ A bottle of wine, please.

☐ A hundred grams of ham, please.

☐ Three hundred grams of mince meat, please.

☐ Two loaves of bread, please.

☐ Three apples, please.

☐ Ten tangerines, please.

▶新潟まで 片道 大人 1枚 ください。
Niigata-made katamichi otona ichi-mai kudasai.

▶新潟まで 片道 子供 1枚 ください。
Niigata-made katamichi kodomo ichi-mai kudasai.

▶長野まで 往復 大人 1枚 ください。
Nagano-made oofuku otona ichi-mai kudasai.

▶長野まで 往復 子供 1枚 ください。
Nagano-made oofuku kodomo ichi-mai kudasai.

▶41円切手 10枚 ください。
Yonjuuichi-en-kitte juu-mai kudasai.

▶はがき 7枚 ください。
Hagaki nana-mai kudasai.

▶36枚どりの フィルム 1本 ください。
Sanjuuroku-mai-dori-no fuirumu ip-pon kudasai.

▶歯ブラシ ください。
Haburashi kudasai.

▶歯みがき ください。
Hamigaki kudasai.

▶たばこ 1箱 ください。
Tabako hito-hako kudasai.

▶ビール 半ダース ください。
Biiru han-daasu kudasai.

▶ワイン 1本 ください。
Wain ip-pon kudasai.

▶ハム 100グラム ください。
Hamu hyaku-guramu kudasai.

▶ひき肉 300グラム ください。
Hikiniku sanbyaku-guramu kudasai.

▶食パン 2斤 ください。
Shokupan ni-kin kudasai.

▶りんご 3つ ください。
Ringo mittsu kudasai.

▶みかん 10個 ください。
Mikan jukko kudasai.

20 ~, please. (2)

Ordering at a restaurant ··························

- [ ] May I see the menu, please?

- [ ] Four No. 15's, please. (*looking at the menu*)

- [ ] Two ham sandwiches, please.

- [ ] One hot dog, please.

- [ ] Two hamburgers and two orders of potatoes, please.

- [ ] Two pork cutlets, please.

- [ ] Three beers, please.

- [ ] Two glasses of whiskey and water, please.

- [ ] A glass of brandy, please.

- [ ] A half bottle of this wine, please.

- [ ] One large Coke, please.

- [ ] Lunch set A, please.

- [ ] The sukiyaki dinner, please.

- [ ] Coffee after the meal, please.

- [ ] One more, please.

・・・

▶メニューを 見せて ください。
Menyuu-o misete-kudasai.

▶15番 4つ ください。
Juugo-ban yottsu kudasai.

▶ハムサンドイッチ 2つ ください。
Hamu-sandoitchi futatsu kudasai.

▶ホットドッグ 1つ ください。
Hottodoggu hitotsu kudasai.

▶ハンバーガー 2つと ポテト 2つ ください。
Hanbaagaa futatsu-to poteto futatsu kudasai.

▶ポークカツ 2つ ください。
Pookukatsu futatsu kudasai.

▶ビール 3つ ください。
Biiru mittsu kudasai.

▶水割りの ウィスキー 2つ ください。
Mizuwari-no uisukii futatsu kudasai.

▶ブランデー ください。
Burandee kudasai.

▶この ワイン, ハーフボトル ください。
Kono wain, haafu-botoru kudasai.

▶コーラの 大きいの 1つ ください。
Koora-no ookii-no hitotsu kudasai.

▶Aランチ 1つ ください。
Ee-ranchi hitotsu kudasai.

▶すきやき定食 ください。
Sukiyaki-teeshoku kudasai.

▶食後に コーヒーを ください。
Shokugo-ni koohii-o kudasai.

▶もう 1つ ください。
Moo hitotsu kudasai.

21 ～, please. (3)

Making requests of someone ·····················

☐ Read me this letter, please.

☐ Write it down here, please.

☐ Say that again, please.

☐ Speak more slowly, please.

☐ Send for a doctor, please.

☐ Be quiet, please.

Making requests at a store / at a bank ···········

☐ Wrap it up, please.

☐ Put it in a bag, please.

☐ Send it, please.

☐ I want to have it cashed, please.

☐ Change it into yen, please.

☐ Give me some small change, please.

Entertaining someone ·····························

☐ Help yourself, please.

☐ Have a seat, please.

☐ Come again, please.

ください (3) Kudasai

▶手紙を 読んでください。
Tegami-o yonde-kudasai.

▶ここに 書いてください。
Koko-ni kaite-kudasai.

▶もう 一度 言ってください。
Moo ichido itte-kudasai.

▶ゆっくり 言ってください。
Yukkuri itte-kudasai.

▶医者を 呼んでください。
Isha-o yonde-kudasai.

▶静かに してください。
Shizuka-ni shite-kudasai.

▶包んでください。
Tsutsunde-kudasai.

▶袋に 入れてください。
Fukuro-ni irete-kudasai.

▶送ってください。
Okutte-kudasai.

▶これを 現金に してください。
Kore-o genkin-ni shite-kudasai.

▶これを 円に してください。
Kore-o en-ni shite-kudasai.

▶これを 小銭に してください。
Kore-o kozeni-ni shite-kudasai.

▶どうぞ 召し上がってください。
Doozo meshiagatte-kudasai.

▶どうぞ おかけください。
Doozo okake-kudasai.

▶また おいでください。
Mata oide-kudasai.

22 No, thank you.

☐ Not for me, thank you.

☐ No, thank you.

☐ No, thank you. I don't smoke.

☐ No, thank you. I don't drink.

☐ No, thank you. I don't like coffee.

☐ No, thank you. I don't like tea.

☐ No, thank you. I don't like milk.

☐ No, thank you. I don't like sweets.

These uses of *Kekkoo-desu* are for when you want to say "No, thank you" to someone's offer of food or drink or something else.

In Japan there are many so-called "family restaurants" that offer *Koohii okawari jiyuu* (free refills of coffee). When the waiter or waitress comes around with a pot of coffee and asks *Koohii-no okawari ikaga-desu-ka* (Would you like some more coffee?), you can refuse by saying *Moo kekkoo-desu*. A note of caution: When saying *kekkoo*, be careful not to put stress on the first syllable; if you do, you will sound extremely abrupt and angry. When you are speaking to a friend or acquaintance, ↗

けっこうです　Kekkoo-desu

▶ 私は けっこうです。
Watashi-wa kekkoo-desu.

▶ もう けっこうです。
Moo kekkoo-desu.

▶ たばこは けっこうです。
Tabako-wa kekkoo-desu.

▶ お酒は けっこうです。
Osake-wa kekkoo-desu.

▶ コーヒーは けっこうです。
Koohii-wa kekkoo-desu.

▶ 紅茶は けっこうです。
Koocha-wa kekkoo-desu.

▶ ミルクは けっこうです。
Miruku-wa kekkoo-desu.

▶ 甘い 物は けっこうです。
Amai mono-wa kekkoo-desu.

⸜you can adjust the phrase a little and say *Arigatoo-gozaimasu, koohii-wa moo kekkoo-desu* (Thank you very much, but I've had enough coffee), or else you can give the reason for refusing, such as *Ima nonde-kita tokoro-desu-node* (I just had some before I came).

Kekkoo is also used as a word of praise, meaning "fine," as in *Kekkoo-na osumai-desu-ne* (What a fine house) and *Sore-de kekkoo-desu* (That's fine). Thus *kekkoo* is known among foreigners as one of those difficult Japanese words which, at first glance, appear to have two completely contradictory meanings. ■

23　Do you know~?/Did you meet~?

People ••

☐ Do you know Mr. Yamamoto?

☐ Do you know that man ?

☐ Did you meet my father?

☐ Did you meet my older brother?

☐ Did you meet my mother?

☐ Did you meet my older sister?

Information •••••••••••••••••••••••••••••••••••••••

☐ Do you know something about Japanese politics?

☐ Do you know something about the Japanese educational system?

☐ Do you know something about Japanese history?

Miscellaneous ••••••••••••••••••••••••••••••••••••••

☐ Do you know when it is?

☐ Do you know where it is?

☐ Do you know who it is?

☐ Do you know why?

ごぞんじですか Gozonji-desu-ka

▶山本さんを ごぞんじですか。
Yamamoto-san-o gozonji-desu-ka.

▶あの 方を ごぞんじですか。
Ano kata-o gozonji-desu-ka.

▶父を ごぞんじですか。
Chichi-o gozonji-desu-ka.

▶兄を ごぞんじですか。
Ani-o gozonji-desu-ka.

▶母を ごぞんじですか。
Haha-o gozonji-desu-ka.

▶姉を ごぞんじですか。
Ane-o gozonji-desu-ka.

▶日本の 政治に ついて ごぞんじですか。
Nihon-no seeji-ni tsuite gozonji-desu-ka.

▶日本の 教育制度に ついて ごぞんじですか。
Nihon-no kyooiku-seedo-ni tsuite gozonji-desu-ka.

▶日本の 歴史に ついて ごぞんじですか。
Nihon-no rekishi-ni tsuite gozonji-desu-ka.

▶それは いつか ごぞんじですか。
Sore-wa itsu-ka gozonji-desu-ka.

▶それは どこか ごぞんじですか。
Sore-wa doko-ka gozonji-desu-ka.

▶それは 誰か ごぞんじですか。
Sore-wa dare-ka gozonji-desu-ka.

▶それは なぜか ごぞんじですか。
Sore-wa naze-ka gozonji-desu-ka.

24 This is ~.

Introducing people ······························

☐ This is my father.

☐ This is my mother.

☐ This is Mr. Yamada.

☐ This is a friend of mine, Mr. Matsumoto.

☐ This is a friend of my father's, Mr. Kawakami.

☐ This is my teacher.

Showing someone around ·····················

☐ This is the cafeteria.

☐ This is the waiting room.

☐ This is the conference room.

☐ This is the lounge.

☐ This is the men's bath.

こちら〜です Kochira 〜desu

・・

▶ こちら 父です。
Kochira chichi-desu.

▶ こちら 母です。
Kochira haha-desu.

▶ こちら 山田さんです。
Kochira Yamada-san-desu.

▶ こちら 友人の 松本さんです。
Kochira yuujin-no Matsumoto-san-desu.

▶ こちら 父の 友人の 川上さんです。
Kochira chichi-no yuujin-no Kawakami-san-desu.

▶ こちら 私の 先生です。
Kochira watashi-no sensee-desu.

・・

▶ こちらが 食堂です。
Kochira-ga shokudoo-desu.

▶ こちらが 控え室です。
Kochira-ga hikaeshitsu-desu.

▶ こちらが 会議室です。
Kochira-ga kaigishitsu-desu.

▶ こちらが 休けい室です。
Kochira-ga kyuukeeshitsu-desu.

▶ こちらが 男性用の 風呂です。
Kochira-ga danseeyoo-no furo-desu.

25　We can't accept that./etc.

Making polite refusals ·····························

☐ We can't accept that.

☐ We can't allow it in here.

☐ We can't do it right now.

☐ You can't make a long distance call.

☐ Please refrain from parking here.

☐ Dogs are not allowed here.

☐ Children are not allowed here.

☐ Please don't take photographs.

Komaru, literally, means "I am perplexed" or "I am in a difficult position because I do not know what I should do." In the uses above, *komaru* is used to convey that permission cannot be granted. If, for example, someone asks *Juugofun-gurai koko-ni kuruma-o tomete-mo ii-desu-ka* (Can I park here for about 15 minutes?), you can deny permission by saying *A, soko-wa komaru-n-desu-ga* (I'm afraid there you be a problem [if you park] there). By saying *komaru*, you are tacitly saying, "You ↗

こまるんですが　Komaru-n-desu-ga

●●●

▶それは　こまるんですが。
Sore-wa komaru-n-desu-ga.

▶ここでは　こまるんですが。
Koko-dewa komaru-n-desu-ga.

▶今 すぐは　こまるんですが。
Ima sugu-wa komaru-n-desu-ga.

▶市外電話は　こまるんですが。
Shigaidenwa-wa komaru-n-desu-ga.

▶無断駐車は　こまるんですが。
Mudanchuusha-wa komaru-n-desu-ga.

▶ペットは　こまるんですが。
Petto-wa komaru-n-desu-ga.

▶子供は　こまるんですが。
Kodomo-wa komaru-n-desu-ga.

▶写真は　こまるんですが。
Shashin-wa komaru-n-desu-ga.

＼can't park there." In the same way, at restaurants one may be told **Petto-wa komaru-n-desu-ga** (Pets are a problem); this means "Pets are not allowed." In Japanese it's customary to avoid saying negative statements directly; **komaru** is a good example of this.

Note that there are other uses of **komaru**, such as **okane-ni komaru** (be pressed for money) and **seekatsu-ni komaru** (have trouble making ends meet). ∎

26 ～ is out of order.

☐ The telephone is out of order.

☐ The refrigerator is out of order.

☐ The camera is out of order.

☐ The radio is out of order.

☐ The television set is out of order.

☐ The air conditioner is out of order.

☐ The heater is out of order.

☐ The oven is out of order.

☐ The gas stove is out of order.

☐ The vacuum cleaner is out of order.

☐ The electric fan is out of order.

☐ The typewriter is out of order.

こわれました　Kowaremashita

▶ 電話が こわれました。
でんわ
Denwa-ga kowaremashita.

▶ 冷蔵庫が こわれました。
れいぞうこ
Reezooko-ga kowaremashita.

▶ カメラが こわれました。
Kamera-ga kowaremashita.

▶ ラジオが こわれました。
Rajio-ga kowaremashita.

▶ テレビが こわれました。
Terebi-ga kowaremashita.

▶ クーラーが こわれました。
Kuuraa-ga kowaremashita.

▶ ヒーターが こわれました。
Hiitaa-ga kowaremashita.

▶ オーブンが こわれました。
Oobun-ga kowaremashita.

▶ ガスコンロが こわれました。
Gasukonro-ga kowaremashita.

▶ 掃除機が こわれました。
そうじき
Soojiki-ga kowaremashita.

▶ 扇風機が こわれました。
せんぷうき
Senpuuki-ga kowaremashita.

▶ タイプライターが こわれました。
Taipuraitaa-ga kowaremashita.

27 May I ask～?/Excuse me, but～?

Asking personal questions ·······················

☐ May I have your name?

☐ May I ask who's calling?

☐ May I have your name?

☐ May I ask who you work for?

☐ May I ask where you go to school?

☐ May I ask where you are from?

☐ May I ask where you live?

☐ May I ask what work you do?

☐ May I ask how large your family is?

☐ May I ask why you came to Japan?

Other questions ·······························

☐ Excuse me, but do you have the time?

☐ Excuse me, but are you Mr. Jackson?

☐ Excuse me, but is this yours?

失礼ですが　Shitsuree-desu-ga

▶失礼ですが　どちらさまですか。
Shitsuree-desu-ga dochirasama-desu-ka.

▶失礼ですが　どちらさまですか。
Shitsuree-desu-ga dochirasama-desu-ka.

▶失礼ですが　お名前は。
Shitsuree-desu-ga onamae-wa.

▶失礼ですが　お勤めは　どちらですか。
Shitsuree-desu-ga otsutome-wa dochira-desu-ka.

▶失礼ですが　学校は　どちらですか。
Shitsuree-desu-ga gakkoo-wa dochira-desu-ka.

▶失礼ですが　お国は　どちらですか。
Shitsuree-desu-ga okuni-wa dochira-desu-ka.

▶失礼ですが　お宅は　どちらですか。
Shitsuree-desu-ga otaku-wa dochira-desu-ka.

▶失礼ですが　どういう　お仕事ですか。
Shitsuree-desu-ga dooyuu oshigoto-desu-ka.

▶失礼ですが　ご家族は　何人ですか。
Shitsuree-desu-ga gokazoku-wa nan-nin-desu-ka.

▶失礼ですが　なぜ　来日　されたのですか。
Shitsuree-desu-ga naze rainichi-sareta-no-desu-ka.

▶失礼ですが　今　何時ですか。
Shitsuree-desu-ga ima nanji-desu-ka.

▶失礼ですが　ジャクソンさんですか。
Shitsuree-desu-ga Jakuson-san-desu-ka.

▶失礼ですが　これは　あなたのですか。
Shitsuree-desu-ga kore-wa anata-no-desu-ka.

28 I like ～. (1)

Food ....

- ☐ I like bread.
- ☐ I like rice.
- ☐ I like fish.
- ☐ I like eggs.
- ☐ I like beef.
- ☐ I like pork.
- ☐ I like chicken.
- ☐ I like ham.
- ☐ I like cheese.
- ☐ I like bacon.
- ☐ I like tomatoes.
- ☐ I like apples.
- ☐ I like bananas.
- ☐ I like cake.
- ☐ I like chocolate.
- ☐ I like sweets.
- ☐ I like ice cream.

● ●

▶パンが すきです。
Pan-ga suki-desu.

▶お米が すきです。
Okome-ga suki-desu.

▶魚が すきです。
Sakana-ga suki-desu.

▶卵が すきです。
Tamago-ga suki-desu.

▶牛肉が すきです。
Gyuuniku-ga suki-desu.

▶豚肉が すきです。
Butaniku-ga suki-desu.

▶鳥肉が すきです。
Toriniku-ga suki-desu.

▶ハムが すきです。
Hamu-ga suki-desu.

▶チーズが すきです。
Chiizu-ga suki-desu.

▶ベーコンが すきです。
Beekon-ga suki-desu.

▶トマトが すきです。
Tomato-ga suki-desu.

▶りんごが すきです。
Ringo-ga suki-desu.

▶バナナが すきです。
Banana-ga suki-desu.

▶ケーキが すきです。
Keeki-ga suki-desu.

▶チョコレートが すきです。
Chokoreeto-ga suki-desu.

▶甘い物が すきです。
Amai mono-ga suki-desu.

▶アイスクリームが すきです。
Aisukuriimu-ga suki-desu.

29 I like ～. (2)

Drinks ••

☐ I like beer.

☐ I like whiskey.

☐ I like Coke.

☐ I like sake.

☐ I like green tea.

☐ I like coffee.

Pastimes •••

☐ I like music.

☐ I like reading.

☐ I like taking pictures.

☐ I like sports.

☐ I like traveling.

☐ I like Japanese ceramics.

☐ I like Japanese dolls.

☐ I like sumo.

☐ I like Kabuki.

すきです ⑵ Suki-desu

▶ ビールが すきです。
Biiru-ga suki-desu.

▶ ウィスキーが すきです。
Uisukii-ga suki-desu.

▶ コーラが すきです。
Koora-ga suki-desu.

▶ 日本酒が すきです。
Nihonshu-ga suki-desu.

▶ 日本茶が すきです。
Nihoncha-ga suki-desu.

▶ コーヒーが すきです。
Koohii-ga suki-desu.

▶ 音楽が すきです。
Ongaku-ga suki-desu.

▶ 読書が すきです。
Dokusho-ga suki-desu.

▶ カメラが すきです。
Kamera-ga suki-desu.

▶ スポーツが すきです。
Supootsu-ga suki-desu.

▶ 旅行が すきです。
Ryokoo-ga suki-desu.

▶ 日本の やきものが すきです。
Nihon-no yakimono-ga suki-desu.

▶ 日本人形が すきです。
Nihon-ningyoo-ga suki-desu.

▶ すもうが すきです。
Sumoo-ga suki-desu.

▶ 歌舞伎が すきです。
Kabuki-ga suki-desu.

30 It's too ~./~ too ~.

☐ It's too large.

☐ It's too small.

☐ It's too expensive.

☐ It's too showy.

☐ It's too plain.

☐ It's too much./ That's too many.

☐ It's too far away.

☐ It's too near.

☐ It's too hard.

☐ It's too dark here.

☐ You work too hard.

☐ You eat too much.

☐ You drink too much.

☐ You sleep too much.

郵便はがき

108-8790

513

料金受取人払

高輪局承認

4586

差出有効期間
平成16年5月
31日まで
〈切手不要〉

〈受取人〉

東京都港区高輪局区内

　芝浦4－5－4

㈱ジャパンタイムズ

出版部愛読者係 行

‖ً‖ً
|‖·ًⓘ·‖·‖ًⓘ·‖·‖ًⓘ·‖·‖·‖·‖·‖·‖·‖·‖·‖·‖·‖·‖·‖‖·‖·‖‖‖|

お名前（ふりがな）		
	男・女	歳

ご職業（学校名）

ご住所 〒

メールアドレス

この本を買った書店名

＊書籍目録をご希望の方は、右の□に✓をつけてください。　　　　□

愛読者はがき（日本語教材）　下の質問にお答えの上、お送りください。

買った本の名前

この本をどのように知りましたか。
　①書店で見て　　　　　　　②広告・書評で見て（雑誌・新聞名　　　　　　）
　③人からすすめられて　　　④ジャパンタイムズのホームページで見て
　⑤学校・先生の指定教材　　⑥その他（　　　　　　　　　　　　　　）

この本をどのように使いますか。
　①個人を教えるため　　　　②クラスで教えるため（生徒数　　　　人）
　③自分で勉強するため　　　④その他（　　　　　　　　　　　　　　　）

この本を買ったのはなぜですか。（いくつでも）
　①レベルや内容がちょうどよいから　　②全体の分量がちょうどよいから
　③テキスト以外の教材もそろっているから　④値段が安いから
　⑤使いやすそうだから　　　　　　　　　⑥著者の名前を知っているから
　⑦その他（　　　　　　　　　　　　　　　　　　　　　　　　　　）

この本を買ったとき、ほかの本とくらべましたか。
　□はい（書名　　　　　　　　　　　　　）　　□いいえ

いままでにジャパンタイムズの日本語教材を買ったことがありますか。
　□はい（書名　　　　　　　　　　　　　）　　□いいえ

この本についてのご意見・ご感想

これからどのような教材が出版されたらいいと思いますか。

どうもありがとうございました。今後の出版の参考にさせていただきます。

～すぎます ～ Sugimasu

▶ それは 大きすぎます。
Sore-wa ooki-sugimasu.

▶ それは 小さすぎます。
Sore-wa chiisa-sugimasu.

▶ それは 高すぎます。
Sore-wa taka-sugimasu.

▶ それは 派手すぎます。
Sore-wa hade-sugimasu.

▶ それは 地味すぎます。
Sore-wa jimi-sugimasu.

▶ それは 多すぎます。
Sore-wa oo-sugimasu.

▶ それは 遠すぎます。
Sore-wa too-sugimasu.

▶ それは 近すぎます。
Sore-wa chika-sugimasu.

▶ それは 難しすぎます。
Sore-wa muzukashi-sugimasu.

▶ ここは 暗すぎます。
Koko-wa kura-sugimasu.

▶ それでは 働きすぎですよ。
Sore-dewa hataraki-sugi-desu-yo.

▶ 食べすぎですよ。
Tabe-sugi-desu-yo.

▶ 飲みすぎですよ。
Nomi-sugi-desu-yo.

▶ 寝すぎですよ。
Ne-sugi-desu-yo.

31 I'm sorry ~.

- [ ] I'm sorry to be late.

- [ ] I'm sorry to have kept you waiting.

- [ ] I'm sorry I have come without warning.

- [ ] I'm sorry to have troubled you so much.

- [ ] I'm sorry to have to change the schedule.

- [ ] I'm sorry I broke it.

- [ ] I'm sorry for bothering you when you're so busy.

- [ ] I'm sorry I haven't seen you for a long time.

- [ ] I'm sorry I couldn't write you sooner.

- [ ] I'm sorry I couldn't tell you beforehand.

- [ ] I'm sorry I couldn't help you.

- [ ] I'm sorry I can't meet you.

- [ ] I'm sorry I can't visit you.

(〜して)すみません (~shite) Sumimasen

▶ 遅くなって すみません。
Osoku-natte sumimasen.

▶ お待たせして すみません。
Omatase-shite sumimasen.

▶ 突然 お邪魔して すみません。
Totsuzen ojama-shite sumimasen.

▶ ご面倒を おかけして すみません。
Gomendoo-o okake-shite sumimasen.

▶ 予定を 変更して すみません。
Yotee-o henkoo-shite sumimasen.

▶ こわしてしまって すみません。
Kowashite-shimatte sumimasen.

▶ お忙しいところ すみません。
Oisogashii-tokoro sumimasen.

▶ ごぶさたして すみません。
Gobusata-shite sumimasen.

▶ お返事が 遅れて すみません。
Ohenji-ga okurete sumimasen.

▶ 事前に 連絡できなくて すみません。
Jizen-ni renraku-dekinakute sumimasen.

▶ お役に 立てなくて すみません。
Oyaku-ni tatenakute sumimasen.

▶ お目に かかれなくて すみません。
Ome-ni kakarenakute sumimasen.

▶ おうかがいできなくて すみません。
Oukagai-dekinakute sumimasen.

32 That's ～.

Expressing agreement ·····························

☐ That's fine.

☐ That's a good idea.

Expressing disagreement ·······················

☐ That's strange.

☐ That's a misunderstanding.

☐ That's impossible.

☐ We can't accept it.

Expressing surprise, sympathy, etc. ···············

☐ That's new to me.

☐ That's a coincidence.

☐ That's too bad.

☐ I didn't know that.

☐ That's unbelievable.

☐ That's a pity.

☐ That's awful.

☐ That's a waste.

☐ I'm sorry to hear that.

それは〜です Sore-wa 〜desu

▶それは よかったですね。
Sore-wa yokatta-desu-ne.

▶それは いい 考えですね。
Sore-wa ii kangae-desu-ne.

▶それは おかしいですよ。
Sore-wa okashii-desu-yo.

▶それは 誤解ですよ。
Sore-wa gokai-desu-yo.

▶それは 無理ですよ。
Sore-wa muri-desu-yo.

▶それは こまりますよ。
Sore-wa komarimasu-yo.

▶それは 初耳ですね。
Sore-wa hatsumimi-desu-ne.

▶それは 偶然の 一致ですね。
Sore-wa guuzen-no itchi-desu-ne.

▶それは いけませんね。
Sore-wa ikemasen-ne.

▶それは 知りませんでした。
Sore-wa shirimasen-deshita.

▶それは 信じられないです。
Sore-wa shinjirarenai-desu.

▶それは かわいそうですね。
Sore-wa kawaisoo-desu-ne.

▶それは ひどいですね。
Sore-wa hidoi-desu-ne.

▶それは もったいないですね。
Sore-wa mottainai-desu-ne.

▶それは 残念ですね。
Sore-wa zannen-desu-ne.

33 I've recovered./We're all right./etc.

On recovering from an illness ·

- ☐ I'm over my cold.

- ☐ I'm over my headache.

- ☐ My stomach is fine now.

- ☐ I'm over my cough.

- ☐ My temperature is normal.

- ☐ I've completely recovered.

Expressing sufficiency ·

- ☐ I've got enough time.

- ☐ I've got enough money.

- ☐ I'm all ready.

- ☐ I'm not hungry.

- ☐ I can do it alone.

Miscellaneous ·

- ☐ This'll do.

- ☐ If you hurry, you can make it.

- ☐ We're all right.

だいじょうぶです　Daijoobu-desu

▶ もう カゼは だいじょうぶです。
Moo kaze-wa daijoobu-desu.

▶ もう 頭痛は だいじょうぶです。
Moo zutsuu-wa daijoobu-desu.

▶ もう おなかは だいじょうぶです。
Moo onaka-wa daijoobu-desu.

▶ もう 咳は だいじょうぶです。
Moo seki-wa daijoobu-desu.

▶ もう 熱は だいじょうぶです。
Moo netsu-wa daijoobu-desu.

▶ もう 体の 方は だいじょうぶです。
Moo karada-no hoo-wa daijoobu-desu.

▶ 時間は だいじょうぶです。
Jikan-wa daijoobu-desu.

▶ お金は だいじょうぶです。
Okane-wa daijoobu-desu.

▶ 準備は だいじょうぶです。
Junbi-wa daijoobu-desu.

▶ おなかは だいじょうぶです。
Onaka-wa daijoobu-desu.

▶ 一人で だいじょうぶです。
Hitori-de daijoobu-desu.

▶ これなら だいじょうぶです。
Kore-nara daijoobu-desu.

▶ 急げば だいじょうぶです。
Isogeba daijoobu-desu.

▶ こちらは だいじょうぶです。
Kochira-wa daijoobu-desu.

34 I want to~. (1)

At the hotel ....

☐ I want to reserve a room.

☐ I want to stay longer.

☐ I want to check out.

☐ I want to check my luggage.

☐ I want to have breakfast in my room.

At the airport ....

☐ I want to make a reservation.

☐ I want to check in.

☐ I want to reconfirm my reservation.

☐ I want to cancel my reservation.

☐ I want to change my flight.

At the store ....

☐ I want to take this.

☐ I want to pay by traveler's check.

☐ I want to exchange this for something else.

☐ I want to exchange this for a different color.

☐ I want to send this.

～(し)たいんですが (1)　~ (Shi)tai-n-desu-ga

▶部屋を 予約したいんですが。
Heya-o yoyaku-shitai-n-desu-ga.

▶滞在を 延ばしたいんですが。
Taizai-o nobashitai-n-desu-ga.

▶チェックアウトしたいんですが。
Chekkuauto-shitai-n-desu-ga.

▶荷物を 一時 預けたいんですが。
Nimotsu-o ichiji azuketai-n-desu-ga.

▶朝食を 部屋で とりたいんですが。
Chooshoku-o heya-de toritai-n-desu-ga.

▶飛行機の 予約を したいんですが。
Hikooki-no yoyaku-o shitai-n-desu-ga.

▶チェックインしたいんですが。
Chekkuin-shitai-n-desu-ga.

▶予約の 再確認を したいんですが。
Yoyaku-no saikakunin-o shitai-n-desu-ga.

▶キャンセルしたいんですが。
Kyanseru-shitai-n-desu-ga.

▶フライトを 変更したいんですが。
Furaito-o henkoo-shitai-n-desu-ga.

▶これを いただきたいんですが。
Kore-o itadakitai-n-desu-ga.

▶トラベラーズチェックで 支払いたいんですが。
Toraberaazu-chekku-de shiharaitai-n-desu-ga.

▶ほかの ものに 替えたいんですが。
Hoka-no mono-ni kaetai-n-desu-ga.

▶別の 色に 替えたいんですが。
Betsu-no iro-ni kaetai-n-desu-ga.

▶送りたいんですが。
Okuritai-n-desu-ga.

35 I want to~. (2)

At the bank ··

☐ I want to have it cashed.

☐ I want to change it into yen.

☐ I want to have some small change.

At the post office ·······························

☐ I want to send this air mail.

☐ I want to send this sea mail.

☐ I want to send a wire.

☐ I want to send it by special delivery.

☐ I want to have it registered.

At the barber's / beauty shop ···············

☐ I want to have a permanent.

☐ I want to have a shampoo and set.

☐ I want to have a haircut.

At the photo store ······························

☐ I want to have this developed.

☐ I want to have this printed.

☐ I want to have this enlarged.

～(し)たいんですが ⑵　～(Shi)tai-n-desu-ga

....

▶現金に したいんですが。
Genkin-ni shitai-n-desu-ga.

▶円に したいんですが。
En-ni shitai-n-desu-ga.

▶小銭に したいんですが。
Kozeni-ni shitai-n-desu-ga.

....

▶これを 航空便で 出したいんですが。
Kore-o kookuubin-de dashitai-n-desu-ga.

▶これを 船便で 送りたいんですが。
Kore-o funabin-de okuritai-n-desu-ga.

▶電報を 打ちたいんですが。
Denpoo-o uchitai-n-desu-ga.

▶速達に したいんですが。
Sokutatsu-ni shitai-n-desu-ga.

▶書留に したいんですが。
Kakitome-ni shitai-n-desu-ga.

....

▶パーマを かけたいんですが。
Paama-o kaketai-n-desu-ga.

▶シャンプーと セットを したいんですが。
Shanpuu-to setto-o shitai-n-desu-ga.

▶カットを したいんですが。
Katto-o shitai-n-desu-ga.

....

▶現像したいんですが。
Genzoo-shitai-n-desu-ga.

▶焼き増ししたいんですが。
Yakimashi-shitai-n-desu-ga.

▶引き伸ばししたいんですが。
Hikinobashi-shitai-n-desu-ga.

36 Just~, please./I'm afraid~./etc.

Making small requests ....

☐ Just a moment, please.

☐ Just take a look, please.

☐ Hold this, please.

☐ Come here, please.

☐ You go first, please.

☐ Let me look at it, please.

☐ Just listen, please.

☐ Lend it to me, please.

☐ Just try it, please.

☐ Just try it on, please.

Turning down requests ....

☐ I'm afraid I'm too busy.

☐ I'm afraid I don't have time.

☐ I'm afraid I can't help you.

☐ I'm afraid I don't know.

☐ I'm afraid I will be late.

☐ I'm afraid he's out now.

ちょっと Chotto

- ▶ちょっと 待ってください。
  Chotto matte-kudasai.
- ▶ちょっと 見てください。
  Chotto mite-kudasai.
- ▶ちょっと 持っていてください。
  Chotto motte-ite-kudasai.
- ▶ちょっと 来てください。
  Chotto kite-kudasai.
- ▶ちょっと 先に 行っていてください。
  Chotto saki-ni itte-ite-kudasai.
- ▶ちょっと 見せてください。
  Chotto misete-kudasai.
- ▶ちょっと 聞いてください。
  Chotto kiite-kudasai.
- ▶ちょっと 貸してください。
  Chotto kashite-kudasai.
- ▶ちょっと 食べてみてください。
  Chotto tabete-mite-kudasai.
- ▶ちょっと 着てみてください。
  Chotto kite-mite-kudasai.

- ▶ちょっと 忙しいんですが。
  Chotto isogashii-n-desu-ga.
- ▶ちょっと 時間が ないんですが。
  Chotto jikan-ga nai-n-desu-ga.
- ▶ちょっと お役に 立てないんですが。
  Chotto oyaku-ni tatenai-n-desu-ga.
- ▶ちょっと わからないんですが。
  Chotto wakaranai-n-desu-ga.
- ▶ちょっと 遅れるんですが。
  Chotto okureru-n-desu-ga.
- ▶ちょっと 今 いないんですが。
  Chotto ima inai-n-desu-ga.

37 Can ~?

☐ Can you make it iced?

☐ Can you make it hot?

☐ Can you make that a set?

☐ Can you make that a large serving?

☐ Can I get it done soon?

☐ Can you do it by tomorrow?

☐ Can you make it earlier?

☐ Can you put it off?

☐ Can you give me a discount on this?

When you go to get a role of film developed you can say *Itsu dekimasu-ka* (When will this be ready?) or *Kyoojuu-ni dekimasu-ka* (Can you have this done by today?). You can also say such things as *Chuugokugo-ga dekimasu* (I can speak Chinese). Thus *dekimasu* is used in many ways to indicate possibility and potential.

So, depending on the context, the phrase *Moo sukoshi hayaku dekimasu-ka* has two possible meanings: "I don't have much time, so please ↗

できますか Dekimasu-ka

▶ アイスに できますか。
Aisu-ni dekimasu-ka.

▶ ホットに できますか。
Hotto-ni dekimasu-ka.

▶ セットに できますか。
Setto-ni dekimasu-ka.

▶ 大盛りに できますか。
Oomori-ni dekimasu-ka.

▶ すぐに できますか。
Sugu-ni dekimasu-ka.

▶ あしたまでに できますか。
Ashita-made-ni dekimasu-ka.

▶ もう すこし 早く できますか。
Moo sukoshi hayaku dekimasu-ka.

▶ もう すこし あとに できますか。
Moo sukoshi ato-ni dekimasu-ka.

▶ もう すこし 安く できますか。
Moo sukoshi yasuku dekimasu-ka.

↘hurry" or "Can you make the time (for the meeting, etc.) a little bit earlier?"

If at a restaurant, you change your mind after ordering, you can ask *Sumimasen, sukiyaki-o onegai-shita-n-desu-ga, ima-kara tenpura-ni dekimasu-ka* (Excuse me, I ordered sukiyaki. Is it too late to change that to tempura?). And the phrase *Nanpun-gurai-de dekimasu-ka* (About how many minutes will it take?) is a good one to remember.

■

38 ~, isn't it?/~, aren't you?

The weather ••••••••••••••••••••••••••••••••••

☐ It's hot today, isn't it?

☐ It's cold today, isn't it?

☐ Nice day today, isn't it?

☐ Bad day today, isn't it?

☐ It's windy today, isn't it?

☐ It's muggy today, isn't it?

☐ It's nice and cool today, isn't it?

☐ It's nice and warm today, isn't it?

Places, people ••••••••••••••••••••••••••••••••

☐ This is the east exit, isn't it?

☐ This is 2-chome, isn't it?

☐ The next stop is Kanda, isn't it?

☐ That's Mr. Hashimoto, isn't it?

☐ That's the teacher, isn't it?

☐ You're an American, aren't you?

☐ You're a clerk here, aren't you?

～ですね (1) ~Desu-ne

▶ きょうは 暑いですね。
Kyoo-wa atsui-desu-ne.

▶ きょうは 寒いですね。
Kyoo-wa samui-desu-ne.

▶ きょうは いい お天気ですね。
Kyoo-wa ii otenki-desu-ne.

▶ きょうは いやな お天気ですね。
Kyoo-wa iya-na otenki-desu-ne.

▶ きょうは 風が 強いですね。
Kyoo-wa kaze-ga tsuyoi-desu-ne.

▶ きょうは むし暑いですね。
Kyoo-wa mushiatsui-desu-ne.

▶ きょうは 涼しいですね。
Kyoo-wa suzushii-desu-ne.

▶ きょうは 暖かいですね。
Kyoo-wa atatakai-desu-ne.

▶ ここは 東口ですね。
Koko-wa higashiguchi-desu-ne.

▶ ここは 2 丁目ですね。
Koko-wa ni-choome-desu-ne.

▶ 次は 神田ですね。
Tsugi-wa Kanda-desu-ne.

▶ あの 方が 橋本さんですね。
Ano kata-ga Hashimoto-san-desu-ne.

▶ あの 方が 先生ですね。
Ano kata-ga sensee-desu-ne.

▶ アメリカの 方ですね。
Amerika-no kata-desu-ne.

▶ お店の 方ですね。
Omise-no kata-desu-ne.

39 It's ~, isn't it?

☐ It's big, isn't it?

☐ It's small, isn't it?

☐ It's light, isn't it?

☐ It's heavy, isn't it?

☐ It's interesting, isn't it?

☐ It's boring, isn't it?

☐ It's dark, isn't it?

☐ It's bright, isn't it?

☐ It's expensive, isn't it?/ It's high, isn't it?

☐ It's cheap, isn't it?

☐ It's low, isn't it?

☐ It's early, isn't it?

☐ It's late, isn't it?

☐ It's fast, isn't it?

☐ It's clean, isn't it?

☐ It's noisy, isn't it?

☐ It's quiet, isn't it?

☐ It's delicious, isn't it?

▶大きいですね。
Ookii-desu-ne.

▶小さいですね。
Chiisai-desu-ne.

▶軽いですね。
Karui-desu-ne.

▶重いですね。
Omoi-desu-ne.

▶おもしろいですね。
Omoshiroi-desu-ne.

▶つまらないですね。
Tsumaranai-desu-ne.

▶暗いですね。
Kurai-desu-ne.

▶明るいですね。
Akarui-desu-ne.

▶高いですね。
Takai-desu-ne.

▶安いですね。
Yasui-desu-ne.

▶低いですね。
Hikui-desu-ne.

▶早いですね。
Hayai-desu-ne.

▶遅いですね。
Osoi-desu-ne.

▶速いですね。
Hayai-desu-ne.

▶きれいですね。
Kiree-desu-ne.

▶うるさいですね。
Urusai-desu-ne.

▶静かですね。
Shizuka-desu-ne.

▶おいしいですね。
Oishii-desu-ne.

40 May I ~?

☐ May I use the telephone?

☐ May I use the bathroom?

☐ May I borrow an umbrella?

☐ May I borrow a pen?

☐ May I borrow this book?

☐ May I borrow a lighter?

☐ May I come in?

☐ May I smoke?

☐ May I sit here?

☐ May I join you?

☐ May I ask a question?

☐ May I come and see you?

☐ May I try it on?

☐ May I interrupt you?

☐ May I take pictures?

☐ May I park here?

☐ May I open the window?

～てもいいですか　～Te-mo ii-desu-ka

▶お電話を お借りしても いいですか。
Odenwa-o okari-shite-mo ii-desu-ka.

▶お手洗いを お借りしても いいですか。
Otearai-o okari-shite-mo ii-desu-ka.

▶傘を お借りしても いいですか。
Kasa-o okari-shite-mo ii-desu-ka.

▶ペンを お借りしても いいですか。
Pen-o okari-shite-mo ii-desu-ka.

▶この 本を お借りしても いいですか。
Kono hon-o okari-shite-mo ii-desu-ka.

▶ライターを お借りしても いいですか。
Raitaa-o okari-shite-mo ii-desu-ka.

▶部屋に 入っても いいですか。
Heya-ni haitte-mo ii-desu-ka.

▶たばこを 吸っても いいですか。
Tabako-o sutte-mo ii-desu-ka.

▶ここに すわっても いいですか。
Koko-ni suwatte-mo ii-desu-ka.

▶ごいっしょしても いいですか。
Goissho-shite-mo ii-desu-ka.

▶質問しても いいですか。
Shitsumon-shite-mo ii-desu-ka.

▶お邪魔しても いいですか。
Ojama-shite-mo ii-desu-ka.

▶着てみても いいですか。
Kite-mite-mo ii-desu-ka.

▶お話し中 失礼しても いいですか。
Ohanashichuu shitsuree-shite-mo ii-desu-ka.

▶写真を とっても いいですか。
Shashin-o totte-mo ii-desu-ka.

▶ここに 駐車しても いいですか。
Koko-ni chuusha-shite-mo ii-desu-ka.

▶窓を 開けても いいですか。
Mado-o akete-mo ii-desu-ka.

41 Why ～?

☐ Why?

☐ Why couldn't you go?

☐ Why couldn't you come?

☐ Why were you late?

☐ Why did you go home?

☐ Why didn't you meet him?

☐ Why didn't you tell me?

☐ Why didn't you buy it?

☐ Why do you hate it so much?

☐ Why are you so sleepy?

☐ Why are you so tired?

☐ Why are you so quiet?

☐ Why are you in such a hurry?

☐ Why is it so expensive?

☐ Why is it so cheap?

☐ Why is it so crowded?

☐ Why is it so empty?

☐ Why is it so popular?

どうして〜ですか　Dooshite 〜desu-ka

▶ どうしてですか。
Dooshite-desu-ka.

▶ どうして 行けなかったんですか。
Dooshite ikenakatta-n-desu-ka.

▶ どうして 来られなかったんですか。
Dooshite korarenakatta-n-desu-ka.

▶ どうして 遅れてしまったんですか。
Dooshite okurete-shimatta-n-desu-ka.

▶ どうして 帰ってしまったんですか。
Dooshite kaette-shimatta-n-desu-ka.

▶ どうして 会わなかったんですか。
Dooshite awanakatta-n-desu-ka.

▶ どうして 言わなかったんですか。
Dooshite iwanakatta-n-desu-ka.

▶ どうして 買わなかったんですか。
Dooshite kawanakatta-n-desu-ka.

▶ どうして そんなに きらいなんですか。
Dooshite sonna-ni kirai-na-n-desu-ka.

▶ どうして そんなに ねむいんですか。
Dooshite sonna-ni nemui-n-desu-ka.

▶ どうして そんなに 疲れているんですか。
Dooshite sonna-ni tsukarete-iru-n-desu-ka.

▶ どうして そんなに 黙っているんですか。
Dooshite sonna-ni damatte-iru-n-desu-ka.

▶ どうして そんなに 急いでいるんですか。
Dooshite sonna-ni isoide-iru-n-desu-ka.

▶ どうして こんなに 高いんですか。
Dooshite konna-ni takai-n-desu-ka.

▶ どうして こんなに 安いんですか。
Dooshite konna-ni yasui-n-desu-ka.

▶ どうして こんなに 混んでいるんですか。
Dooshite konna-ni konde-iru-n-desu-ka.

▶ どうして こんなに すいているんですか。
Dooshite konna-ni suite-iru-n-desu-ka.

▶ どうして そんなに 人気が あるんですか。
Dooshite sonna-ni ninki-ga aru-n-desu-ka.

~, please. / Have ~, please.

Inviting people in ·····································

☐ Come in, please.

☐ Come here, please.

☐ May I take your coat, please?

☐ Make yourself at home, please.

☐ Help yourself, please.

☐ Take a look, please.

☐ Have a seat, please.

Offering refreshments ·····························

☐ Have a cigarette, please.

☐ Have a cup of coffee, please.

☐ Have a glass of beer, please.

☐ Have some fruit, please.

☐ Have some sandwiches, please.

☐ Have some more, please.

☐ Have a little more, please.

☐ Have one, please.

☐ Help yourself, please.

どうぞ Doozo

▶ どうぞ お入りください。
Doozo ohairi-kudasai.

▶ どうぞ こちらへ おいでください。
Doozo kochira-e oide-kudasai.

▶ どうぞ コートを お取りください。
Doozo kooto-o otori-kudasai.

▶ どうぞ おくつろぎください。
Doozo okutsurogi-kudasai.

▶ どうぞ お持ちください。
Doozo omochi-kudasai.

▶ どうぞ ご覧ください。
Doozo goran-kudasai.

▶ どうぞ おかけください。
Doozo okake-kudasai.

▶ たばこを 一本 どうぞ。
Tabako-o ippon doozo.

▶ コーヒーを どうぞ。
Koohii-o doozo.

▶ ビールを どうぞ。
Biiru-o doozo.

▶ くだものを どうぞ。
Kudamono-o doozo.

▶ サンドイッチを どうぞ。
Sandoitchi-o doozo.

▶ お代わりを どうぞ。
Okawari-o doozo.

▶ もう すこし どうぞ。
Moo sukoshi doozo.

▶ どうぞ ひとつ お取りください。
Doozo hitotsu otori-kudasai.

▶ どうぞ お召し上がりください。
Doozo omeshiagari-kudasai.

43 Please tell me how to ~.

☐ Please tell me how to do it.

☐ Please tell me how to go there.

☐ Please tell me how to go home.

☐ Please tell me how to open it.

☐ Please tell me how to close it.

☐ Please tell me how to use it.

☐ Please tell me how to pronounce it.

☐ Please tell me how to buy it.

☐ Please tell me how to make it.

☐ Please tell me how to eat it.

☐ Please tell me how to reserve it.

☐ Please tell me how to cancel it.

☐ Please tell me how to put it on.

☐ Please tell me how to turn it on.

☐ Please tell me how to turn it off.

どうやって　Doo yatte

▶ どう やって やるんですか。
Doo yatte yaru-n-desu-ka.

▶ どう やって 行くんですか。
Doo yatte iku-n-desu-ka.

▶ どう やって 帰るんですか。
Doo yatte kaeru-n-desu-ka.

▶ どう やって 開けるんですか。
Doo yatte akeru-n-desu-ka.

▶ どう やって 閉めるんですか。
Doo yatte shimeru-n-desu-ka.

▶ どう やって 使うんですか。
Doo yatte tsukau-n-desu-ka.

▶ どう やって 発音するんですか。
Doo yatte hatsuon-suru-n-desu-ka.

▶ どう やって 買うんですか。
Doo yatte kau-n-desu-ka.

▶ どう やって 作るんですか。
Doo yatte tsukuru-n-desu-ka.

▶ どう やって 食べるんですか。
Doo yatte taberu-n-desu-ka.

▶ どう やって 予約を するんですか。
Doo yatte yoyaku-o suru-n-desu-ka.

▶ どう やって 取り消すんですか。
Doo yatte torikesu-n-desu-ka.

▶ どう やって 着るんですか。
Doo yatte kiru-n-desu-ka.

▶ どう やって つけるんですか。
Doo yatte tsukeru-n-desu-ka.

▶ どう やって 消すんですか。
Doo yatte kesu-n-desu-ka.

44 Which ～?

□ Which is cheaper?

□ Which is better?

□ Which is more interesting?

□ Which is more delicious?

□ Which do you like best?

□ Which is more difficult?

□ Which is easier?

□ Which is more convenient?

□ Which one is there more of?

□ Which is colder?

□ Which is hotter?

□ Which is faster?

□ Which is more quiet?

どちら(の方)が　Dochira(-no hoo)-ga

▶ どちら(の 方)が 安いですか。
Dochira(-no hoo)-ga yasui-desu-ka.

▶ どちら(の 方)が いいですか。
Dochira(-no hoo)-ga ii-desu-ka.

▶ どちら(の 方)が おもしろいですか。
Dochira(-no hoo)-ga omoshiroi-desu-ka.

▶ どちら(の 方)が おいしいですか。
Dochira(-no hoo)-ga oishii-desu-ka.

▶ どちら(の 方)が おすきですか。
Dochira(-no hoo)-ga osuki-desu-ka.

▶ どちら(の 方)が 難しいですか。
Dochira(-no hoo)-ga muzukashii-desu-ka.

▶ どちら(の 方)が 簡単ですか。
Dochira(-no hoo)-ga kantan-desu-ka.

▶ どちら(の 方)が 便利ですか。
Dochira(-no hoo)-ga benri-desu-ka.

▶ どちら(の 方)が 多いですか。
Dochira(-no hoo)-ga ooi-desu-ka.

▶ どちら(の 方)が 寒いですか。
Dochira(-no hoo)-ga samui-desu-ka.

▶ どちら(の 方)が 暑いですか。
Dochira(-no hoo)-ga atsui-desu-ka.

▶ どちら(の 方)が 速いですか。
Dochira(-no hoo)-ga hayai-desu-ka.

▶ どちら(の 方)が 静かですか。
Dochira(-no hoo)-ga shizuka-desu-ka.

45 Where is ∼? (1)

At a hotel ·······················

☐ Where is the front desk?

☐ Where is the grill?

☐ Where is the bar?

☐ Where's the money exchange?

At the station ·······················

☐ Where's the ticket office?

☐ Where is the lost and found?

☐ Where is the rest room?

☐ Where can we take a taxi?

☐ Where is track No. 13?

☐ Where is the east exit?

At the airport ·······················

☐ Where is the bank?

☐ Where is the souvenir shop?

☐ Where is the baggage claim?

☐ Where is the bus stop?

☐ Where is the Japan Air Lines counter?

どちらですか (1) Dochira-desu-ka

▶ フロントは どちらですか。
Furonto-wa dochira-desu-ka.

▶ 食堂は どちらですか。
Shokudoo-wa dochira-desu-ka.

▶ バーは どちらですか。
Baa-wa dochira-desu-ka.

▶ 両替所は どちらですか。
Ryoogaejo-wa dochira-desu-ka.

▶ 切符売り場は どちらですか。
Kippu-uriba-wa dochira-desu-ka.

▶ 遺失物係は どちらですか。
Ishitsubutsugakari-wa dochira-desu-ka.

▶ お手洗いは どちらですか。
Otearai-wa dochira-desu-ka.

▶ タクシー乗り場は どちらですか。
Takushii-noriba-wa dochira-desu-ka.

▶ 13番線は どちらですか。
Juusan-bansen-wa dochira-desu-ka.

▶ 東口は どちらですか。
Higashiguchi-wa dochira-desu-ka.

▶ 銀行は どちらですか。
Ginkoo-wa dochira-desu-ka.

▶ 売店は どちらですか。
Baiten-wa dochira-desu-ka.

▶ 手荷物預り所は どちらですか。
Tenimotsu-azukarijo-wa dochira-desu-ka.

▶ バス乗り場は どちらですか。
Basu-noriba-wa dochira-desu-ka.

▶ 日本航空の カウンターは どちらですか。
Nihonkookuu-no kauntaa-wa dochira-desu-ka.

46 Where is ~? (2)

Other places ....

☐ Where is the parking lot?

☐ Where is the entrance?

☐ Where is the exit?

☐ Where is the cashier?

☐ Where is the elevator?

☐ Where is the hospital?

☐ Where is the post office?

☐ Where is the bank?

☐ Where is the police station?

☐ Where is the American Embassy?

☐ Where is the gas station?

Asking personal questions ....

☐ Where were you born?

☐ Where are you from?

☐ Who do you work for?

☐ Where do you go to school?

☐ Where do you live?

● ●

▶ 駐車場は どちらですか。
Chuushajoo-wa dochira-desu-ka.

▶ 入口は どちらですか。
Iriguchi-wa dochira-desu-ka.

▶ 出口は どちらですか。
Deguchi-wa dochira-desu-ka.

▶ レジは どちらですか。
Reji-wa dochira-desu-ka.

▶ エレベーターは どちらですか。
Erebeetaa-wa dochira-desu-ka.

▶ 病院は どちらですか。
Byooin-wa dochira-desu-ka.

▶ 郵便局は どちらですか。
Yuubinkyoku-wa dochira-desu-ka.

▶ 銀行は どちらですか。
Ginkoo-wa dochira-desu-ka.

▶ 交番は どちらですか。
Kooban-wa dochira-desu-ka.

▶ アメリカ大使館は どちらですか。
Amerika-taishikan-wa dochira-desu-ka.

▶ ガソリンスタンドは どちらですか。
Gasorinsutando-wa dochira-desu-ka.

● ●

▶ お生まれは どちらですか。
Oumare-wa dochira-desu-ka.

▶ お国は どちらですか。
Okuni-wa dochira-desu-ka.

▶ お勤めは どちらですか。
Otsutome-wa dochira-desu-ka.

▶ 学校は どちらですか。
Gakkoo-wa dochira-desu-ka.

▶ お宅は どちらですか。
Otaku-wa dochira-desu-ka.

47 Where ~?

☐ Where are you going? (*to someone going out*)

☐ Where are you going? (*to someone going home*)

☐ Where are you going to stay?

☐ Where shall I take this?

☐ Where shall I send this?

☐ Who shall I hand it over to?

☐ Where shall I meet you?

☐ Where shall I deliver this?

We have seen quite a few phrases that use *dochira*. Section 44 covers comparisons, but what about when you want to compare, say, object A and object B? For that, use a phrase like the following: *Kore-to sore-to dochira-no hoo-ga takai-desu-ka* (This or that—which is more expensive?). You can use this pattern if the objects of comparison are things, people, places, etc. *Dochira* here is the polite form of *dotchi*. Among friends you would say, for example, *Dotchi-ga ii* (Which is better?).

Sections 45 through 47 introduce phrases in which *dochira* means "where." In these cases *dochira* is the polite form for *doko* (where). Thus ~*wa dochira-desu-ka* is simply a polite way of saying ~*wa doko-desu-ka* (Where is ~?). ↗

どちらへ Dochira-e

▶ どちらへ お出かけですか。
Dochira-e odekake-desu-ka.

▶ どちらへ お帰りですか。
Dochira-e okaeri-desu-ka.

▶ どちらへ お泊まりですか。
Dochira-e otomari-desu-ka.

▶ どちらへ お持ちしますか。
Dochira-e omochi-shimasu-ka.

▶ どちらへ お送りしますか。
Dochira-e ookuri-shimasu-ka.

▶ どちらへ お渡ししますか。
Dochira-e owatashi-shimasu-ka.

▶ どちらへ お迎えに 上がりますか。
Dochira-e omukae-ni agarimasu-ka.

▶ どちらへ お届けしますか。
Dochira-e otodoke-shimasu-ka.

↘ Depending on the context, though, it can also be asking not so much where something is, but rather which is the right direction: *Suimasen, eki-wa dochira-desu-ka* (Excuse me, which way is the station?) — *Kono michi-o massugu-desu-yo* (It's straight up this street).

In section 47, all the sentences start with *dochira* and end with a verb that is in an honorific form. People who meet, for example, while traveling will speak to each other in this polite way, and will ask each other questions like *Dochira-kara irasshatta-n-desu-ka* (Where are you from?) and *Dochira-made irassharu-n-desu-ka* (Where are you traveling to?).

■

48 How much/many/long/etc.~?

☐ How long does it take?/How much does it cost?

☐ How many do you need?/How much do you need?

☐ How much do you eat?

☐ How much do you drink?

☐ How far is it from here?

☐ What's the population?

☐ How much is the admission fee?

☐ How much is the charge?

☐ How much is the fare?

☐ How much is the tuition?

☐ How much is the membership fee?

☐ How much is the salary?

☐ How much is the tax?

☐ How much is the service charge?

☐ How much is the electric bill?

☐ How much is the telephone bill?

☐ How much is the rent?

どのくらい　Dono-kurai

▶ どのくらい　かかりますか。
Dono-kurai kakarimasu-ka.

▶ どのくらい　いりますか。
Dono-kurai irimasu-ka.

▶ どのくらい　食べますか。
Dono-kurai tabemasu-ka.

▶ どのくらい　飲みますか。
Dono-kurai nomimasu-ka.

▶ 距離は　どのくらいですか。
Kyori-wa dono-kurai-desu-ka.

▶ 人口は　どのくらいですか。
Jinkoo-wa dono-kurai-desu-ka.

▶ 入場料は　どのくらいですか。
Nyuujooryoo-wa dono-kurai-desu-ka.

▶ 料金は　どのくらいですか。
Ryookin-wa dono-kurai-desu-ka.

▶ 運賃は　どのくらいですか。
Unchin-wa dono-kurai-desu-ka.

▶ 授業料は　どのくらいですか。
Jugyooryoo-wa dono-kurai-desu-ka.

▶ 会費は　どのくらいですか。
Kaihi-wa dono-kurai-desu-ka.

▶ 給料は　どのくらいですか。
Kyuuryoo-wa dono-kurai-desu-ka.

▶ 税金は　どのくらいですか。
Zeekin-wa dono-kurai-desu-ka.

▶ サービス料は　どのくらいですか。
Saabisuryoo-wa dono-kurai-desu-ka.

▶ 電気代は　どのくらいですか。
Denkidai-wa dono-kurai-desu-ka.

▶ 電話代は　どのくらいですか。
Denwadai-wa dono-kurai-desu-ka.

▶ 家賃は　どのくらいですか。
Yachin-wa dono-kurai-desu-ka.

49 Please don't ~.

☐ Please don't come in.

☐ Please don't go out.

☐ Please be quiet.

☐ Please stop fighting.

☐ Please keep your hands off.

☐ Please don't eat too much.

☐ Please don't drink too much.

☐ Please don't smoke too much.

☐ Please don't sit up late at night.

☐ Please take your shoes off.

You will often see the pattern ~*naide-kudasai* on signs and hear it over public address systems; it is a common way of indicating what is prohibited. On buses you'll often hear announcements like *Mado-kara te-ya kao-o dasanaide-kudasai* (Please don't stick your hand or head out the window), and at exhibits you'll often see signs like *Sakuhin-ni te-o furenaide-kudasai* (Please don't touch the pieces). Other phrases you'll hear are *Tabako-wa oyame-kudasai* (Please don't smoke), and *Kakekomi-joosha-wa oyame-kudasai* ↗

～ないでください ～Naide-kudasai

▶中に 入らないでください。
Naka-ni hairanaide-kudasai.

▶外に 出ないでください。
Soto-ni denaide-kudasai.

▶騒がないでください。
Sawaganaide-kudasai.

▶けんかを しないでください。
Kenka-o shinaide-kudasai.

▶さわらないでください。
Sawaranaide-kudasai.

▶あまり 食べないでください。
Amari tabenaide-kudasai.

▶あまり お酒を 飲まないでください。
Amari osake-o nomanaide-kudasai.

▶あまり たばこを 吸わないでください。
Amari tabako-o suwanaide-kudasai.

▶夜ふかしを しないでください。
Yofukashi-o shinaide-kudasai.

▶土足で 上がらないでください。
Dosoku-de agaranaide-kudasai.

↘(Please don't rush onto the trains).

This pattern is a little less strict than ～*shite-wa ikemasen* (You mustn't do ～). Even so, if you use ～*naide-kudasai* among friends or acquaintances you will sound rather harsh, so be careful. So if a friend asks you *Yoru odenwa-shite-mo ii-desu-ka* (May I call you at night?), avoid saying *Shinaide-kudasai* (Don't). It's better to say something indirect, like, *Sumimasen-kedo, yoru-wa chotto...* (I'm sorry, but night's a little...) Your friend will understand exactly what you mean. ■

50 I lost ∼.

☐ I lost my umbrella.

☐ I lost my glasses.

☐ I lost my hat.

☐ I lost my camera.

☐ I lost my watch.

☐ I lost my fountain pen.

☐ I lost my suitcase.

☐ I lost my handbag.

☐ I lost my passport.

☐ I lost my wallet.

☐ I lost my coin purse.

☐ I lost my key.

☐ I lost my I.D. card.

☐ I lost my driver's license.

なくしました Nakushimashita

▶ 傘を なくしました。
Kasa-o nakushimashita.

▶ メガネを なくしました。
Megane-o nakushimashita.

▶ 帽子を なくしました。
Booshi-o nakushimashita.

▶ カメラを なくしました。
Kamera-o nakushimashita.

▶ 時計を なくしました。
Tokee-o nakushimashita.

▶ 万年筆を なくしました。
Mannenhitsu-o nakushimashita.

▶ スーツケースを なくしました。
Suutsukeesu-o nakushimashita.

▶ ハンドバッグを なくしました。
Handobaggu-o nakushimashita.

▶ パスポートを なくしました。
Pasupooto-o nakushimashita.

▶ 財布を なくしました。
Saifu-o nakushimashita.

▶ 小銭入れを なくしました。
Kozeniire-o nakushimashita.

▶ 鍵を なくしました。
Kagi-o nakushimashita.

▶ 身分証明書を なくしました。
Mibunshoomeesho-o nakushimashita.

▶ 免許証を なくしました。
Menkyoshoo-o nakushimashita.

51 I must ~.

- ☐ I must go now.

- ☐ I must go to bed now.

- ☐ I must stop for now.

- ☐ I must go to work now.

- ☐ I must study.

- ☐ I must stay home.

- ☐ I must make a phone call.

- ☐ I must write a letter.

- ☐ I must do the washing.

- ☐ I must clean the house.

- ☐ I must go shopping.

- ☐ I must go to the hospital.

- ☐ I must go to the dentist.

- ☐ I must go to the barbershop.

- ☐ I must go to the hairdresser's.

- ☐ I must pick up my children.

～なりません ～Narimasen

▶ もう 行かなければ なりません。
Moo ikanakereba narimasen.

▶ もう 寝なければ なりません。
Moo nenakereba narimasen.

▶ もう やめなければ なりません。
Moo yamenakereba narimasen.

▶ もう 仕事に 行かなければなりません。
Moo shigoto-ni ikanakereba narimasen.

▶ 勉強しなければ なりません。
Benkyoo-shinakereba narimasen.

▶ 家に いなければ なりません。
Ie-ni inakereba narimasen.

▶ 電話を かけなければ なりません。
Denwa-o kakenakereba narimasen.

▶ 手紙を 書かなければ なりません。
Tegami-o kakanakereba narimasen.

▶ 洗濯を しなければ なりません。
Sentaku-o shinakereba narimasen.

▶ 掃除を しなければ なりません。
Sooji-o shinakereba narimasen.

▶ 買い物に 行かなければ なりません。
Kaimono-ni ikanakereba narimasen.

▶ 病院に 行かなければ なりません。
Byooin-ni ikanakereba narimasen.

▶ 歯医者に 行かなければ なりません。
Haisha-ni ikanakereba narimasen.

▶ 床屋に 行かなければ なりません。
Tokoya-ni ikanakereba narimasen.

▶ 美容院に 行かなければ なりません。
Biyooin-ni ikanakereba narimasen.

▶ 子供を 迎えに 行かなければ なりません。
Kodomo-o mukae-ni ikanakereba narimasen.

52 What ~?

☐ What's that? / What are those?

☐ What's this? / What are these?

☐ What is it? / What are they?

☐ What's that big building?

☐ What's that crowd?

☐ What's that notice?

☐ What's your job?

☐ What's your hobby?

☐ What's your favorite food?

☐ What's your favorite drink?

☐ What's your major?

☐ What's your blood type?

なんですか **Nan-desu-ka**

▶ あれは なんですか。
Are-wa nan-desu-ka.

▶ これは なんですか。
Kore-wa nan-desu-ka.

▶ それは なんですか。
Sore-wa nan-desu-ka.

▶ あの 大きい 建物は なんですか。
Ano ookii tatemono-wa nan-desu-ka.

▶ あの 人だかりは なんですか。
Ano hitodakari-wa nan-desu-ka.

▶ あの 掲示は なんですか。
Ano keeji-wa nan-desu-ka.

▶ お仕事は なんですか。
Oshigoto-wa nan-desu-ka.

▶ ご趣味は なんですか。
Goshumi-wa nan-desu-ka.

▶ おすきな 食べ物は なんですか。
Osuki-na tabemono-wa nan-desu-ka.

▶ おすきな 飲み物は なんですか。
Osuki-na nomimono-wa nan-desu-ka.

▶ ご専門は なんですか。
Gosenmon-wa nan-desu-ka.

▶ 血液型は なんですか。
Ketsuekigata-wa nan-desu-ka.

53 I'll take ~./I'll ride ~.

- [ ] I'll take a bus.

- [ ] I'll take a sightseeing bus.

- [ ] I'll take a taxi.

- [ ] I'll take a train.

- [ ] I'll take a subway.

- [ ] I'll take a plane.

- [ ] I'll take the monorail.

- [ ] I'll take a ship.

- [ ] I'll ride a bicycle.

- [ ] I'll ride a horse.

- [ ] I'll ride a motorbike.

- [ ] I'll take a cable car.

- [ ] I'll take the elevator.

- [ ] I'll take the escalator.

のります Norimasu

▶ バスに のります。
Basu-ni norimasu.

▶ 観光バスに のります。
Kankoobasu-ni norimasu.

▶ タクシーに のります。
Takushii-ni norimasu.

▶ 電車に のります。
Densha-ni norimasu.

▶ 地下鉄に のります。
Chikatetsu-ni norimasu.

▶ 飛行機に のります。
Hikooki-ni norimasu.

▶ モノレールに のります。
Monoreeru-ni norimasu.

▶ 船に のります。
Fune-ni norimasu.

▶ 自転車に のります。
Jitensha-ni norimasu.

▶ 馬に のります。
Uma-ni norimasu.

▶ オートバイに のります。
Ootobai-ni norimasu.

▶ ケーブルカーに のります。
Keeburukaa-ni norimasu.

▶ エレベーターに のります。
Erebeetaa-ni norimasu.

▶ エスカレーターに のります。
Esukareetaa-ni norimasu.

54 I want ～./I'd like ～.

- [ ] I want that one.

- [ ] I want this one.

- [ ] I want a larger one.

- [ ] I want a smaller one.

- [ ] I'd like you to help me.

- [ ] I'd like you to wait here.

- [ ] I'd like you to write me.

- [ ] I'd like this delivered.

- [ ] I'd like this sent.

- [ ] I'd like this fixed.

- [ ] I'd like this brought to my room.

- [ ] I'd like you to come get it.

- [ ] I'd like you to come here now.

ほしいんですが　Hoshii-n-desu-ga

▶ あれが ほしいんですが。
Are-ga hoshii-n-desu-ga.

▶ これが ほしいんですが。
Kore-ga hoshii-n-desu-ga.

▶ もっと 大きい サイズが ほしいんですが。
Motto ookii saizu-ga hoshii-n-desu-ga.

▶ もっと 小さい サイズが ほしいんですが。
Motto chiisai saizu-ga hoshii-n-desu-ga.

▶ 手伝って ほしいんですが。
Tetsudatte hoshii-n-desu-ga.

▶ ここで 待っていて ほしいんですが。
Koko-de matte-ite hoshii-n-desu-ga.

▶ 手紙を 書いて ほしいんですが。
Tegami-o kaite hoshii-n-desu-ga.

▶ 届けて ほしいんですが。
Todokete hoshii-n-desu-ga.

▶ 送って ほしいんですが。
Okutte hoshii-n-desu-ga.

▶ 直して ほしいんですが。
Naoshite hoshii-n-desu-ga.

▶ 部屋に 持ってきて ほしいんですが。
Heya-ni motte-kite hoshii-n-desu-ga.

▶ 取りに 来て ほしいんですが。
Tori-ni kite hoshii-n-desu-ga.

▶ すぐに 来て ほしいんですが。
Sugu-ni kite hoshii-n-desu-ga.

55 Let's~.

☐ Let's go.

☐ Let's wait.

☐ Let's have a seat.

☐ Let's take a taxi.

☐ Let's take a bus.

☐ Let's take a train.

☐ Let's go by subway.

☐ Let's have a drink.

☐ Let's have a meal.

☐ Let's take a rest.

☐ Let's go to the movies.

☐ Let's go for a drive.

☐ Let's go shopping.

☐ Let's go swimming.

☐ Let's go skiing.

☐ Let's go on a picnic.

☐ Let's go golfing.

☐ Let's go bowling.

～ましょう ～Mashoo

▶ 出かけましょう。
Dekakemashoo.

▶ 待ちましょう。
Machimashoo.

▶ すわりましょう。
Suwarimashoo.

▶ タクシーを 拾いましょう。
Takushii-o hiroimashoo.

▶ バスで 行きましょう。
Basu-de ikimashoo.

▶ 電車で 行きましょう。
Densha-de ikimashoo.

▶ 地下鉄で 行きましょう。
Chikatetsu-de ikimashoo.

▶ 一杯 やりましょう。
Ippai yarimashoo.

▶ 食事に しましょう。
Shokuji-ni shimashoo.

▶ ひと休み しましょう。
Hitoyasumi shimashoo.

▶ 映画に 行きましょう。
Eega-ni ikimashoo.

▶ ドライブに 行きましょう。
Doraibu-ni ikimashoo.

▶ 買い物に 行きましょう。
Kaimono-ni ikimashoo.

▶ 泳ぎに 行きましょう。
Oyogi-ni ikimashoo.

▶ スキーに 行きましょう。
Sukii-ni ikimashoo.

▶ ピクニックに 行きましょう。
Pikunikku-ni ikimashoo.

▶ ゴルフに 行きましょう。
Gorufu-ni ikimashoo.

▶ ボーリングに 行きましょう。
Booringu-ni ikimashoo.

56 Shall we ～?

☐ Shall we go for a walk?

☐ Shall we go out to dinner?

☐ Shall we bowl?

☐ Shall we play cards?

☐ Shall we skate?

☐ Shall we dance?

☐ Shall we play catch?

☐ Shall we play golf?

☐ Shall we go for a drive?

☐ Shall we go to a movie?

☐ Shall we go skiing?

☐ Shall we go to a baseball game?

☐ Shall we go fishing?

〜ませんか 〜Masen-ka

▶散歩 しませんか。
Sanpo shimasen-ka.

▶いっしょに 食事 しませんか。
Issho-ni shokuji shimasen-ka.

▶ボーリング しませんか。
Booringu shimasen-ka.

▶トランプ しませんか。
Toranpu shimasen-ka.

▶スケート しませんか。
Sukeeto shimasen-ka.

▶ダンス しませんか。
Dansu shimasen-ka.

▶キャッチボール しませんか。
Kyatchibooru shimasen-ka.

▶ゴルフ しませんか。
Gorufu shimasen-ka.

▶ドライブ しませんか。
Doraibu shimasen-ka.

▶映画に 行きませんか。
Eega-ni ikimasen-ka.

▶スキーに 行きませんか。
Sukii-ni ikimasen-ka.

▶野球に 行きませんか。
Yakyuu-ni ikimasen-ka.

▶釣りに 行きませんか。
Tsuri-ni ikimasen-ka.

57 Please show me ~.

☐ Please show it to me.

☐ Please show me a cheaper one.

☐ Please show me a more expensive one.

☐ Please show me a larger one.

☐ Please show me a smaller one.

☐ Please show me another one.

☐ Please show me that in another color.

☐ Please show me a sample.

☐ Please show me the real one.

☐ Please show me the whole thing.

☐ Please show me some ties.

☐ Please show me some handkerchiefs.

☐ Please show me some socks.

☐ Please show me some white shirts.

☐ Please show me some pants.

☐ Please show me some jackets.

☐ Please show me some skirts.

☐ Please show me some blouses.

▶ あれを 見せてください。
Are-o misete-kudasai.

▶ もっと 安いのを 見せてください。
Motto yasui-no-o misete-kudasai.

▶ もっと 高いのを 見せてください。
Motto takai-no-o misete-kudasai.

▶ もっと 大きいのを 見せてください。
Motto ookii-no-o misete-kudasai.

▶ もっと 小さいのを 見せてください。
Motto chiisai-no-o misete-kudasai.

▶ ほかのを 見せてください。
Hoka-no-o misete-kudasai.

▶ ほかの 色のを 見せてください。
Hoka-no iro-no-o misete-kudasai.

▶ 見本を 見せてください。
Mihon-o misete-kudasai.

▶ 実物を 見せてください。
Jitsubutsu-o misete-kudasai.

▶ 全部 見せてください。
Zenbu misete-kudasai.

▶ ネクタイを 見せてください。
Nekutai-o misete-kudasai.

▶ ハンカチを 見せてください。
Hankachi-o misete-kudasai.

▶ 靴下を 見せてください。
Kutsushita-o misete-kudasai.

▶ ワイシャツを 見せてください。
Waishatsu-o misete-kudasai.

▶ ズボンを 見せてください。
Zubon-o misete-kudasai.

▶ 上着を 見せてください。
Uwagi-o misete-kudasai.

▶ スカートを 見せてください。
Sukaato-o misete-kudasai.

▶ ブラウスを 見せてください。
Burausu-o misete-kudasai.

58 May I see ～?

☐ May I see your I.D. card?

☐ May I see your ticket?

☐ May I see your passport?

☐ May I see your boarding pass?

☐ May I see the ticket stub?

☐ May I see the menu?

☐ May I see the price list?

☐ May I see the pamphlet?

☐ May I see the catalog?

☐ May I see a guide-book?

☐ May I see the seat plan?

☐ May I see the schedule?

☐ May I see a city map?

☐ May I use the telephone directory?

☐ May I see the bill?

☐ May I see the specifications?

見せてください (2)　Misete-kudasai

▶ 身分証明書を 見せてください。
Mibunshoomeesho-o misete-kudasai.

▶ 切符を 見せてください。
Kippu-o misete-kudasai.

▶ パスポートを 見せてください。
Pasupooto-o misete-kudasai.

▶ 搭乗券を 見せてください。
Toojooken-o misete-kudasai.

▶ 半券を 見せてください。
hanken-o misete-kudasai.

▶ メニューを 見せてください。
Menyuu-o misete-kudasai.

▶ 値段表を 見せてください。
Nedanhyoo-o misete-kudasai.

▶ パンフレットを 見せてください。
Panfuretto-o misete-kudasai.

▶ カタログを 見せてください。
Katarogu-o misete-kudasai.

▶ 案内書を 見せてください。
Annaisho-o misete-kudasai.

▶ 座席表を 見せてください。
Zasekihyoo-o misete-kudasai.

▶ 時間表を 見せてください。
Jikanhyoo-o misete-kudasai.

▶ 地図を 見せてください。
Chizu-o misete-kudasai.

▶ 電話帳を 見せてください。
Denwachoo-o misete-kudasai.

▶ 請求書を 見せてください。
Seekyuusho-o misete-kudasai.

▶ 使用説明書を 見せてください。
Shiyoosetsumeesho-o misete-kudasai.

59 That's enough./It's time~./etc.

When you've had enough ··························

☐ I've had enough.

☐ That's enough.

☐ No, thank you.

When you're ready to give up ·····················

☐ Let's stop already.

☐ I give up.

☐ I can't wait any longer.

☐ I can't stand it any longer.

☐ Let's give up.

When it's time to do something ··················

☐ It'll be done soon.

☐ I'm about to leave.

☐ It's time you went to bed.

☐ It's time you had a meal.

☐ It's departure time.

☐ It's time to assemble.

☐ It has already begun.

もう Moo

▶ もう いりません。
Moo irimasen.

▶ もう いいです。
Moo ii-desu.

▶ もう けっこうです。
Moo kekkoo-desu.

▶ もう やめましょう。
Moo yamemashoo.

▶ もう だめです。
Moo dame-desu.

▶ もう 待てません。
Moo matemasen.

▶ もう がまんできません。
Moo gaman-dekimasen.

▶ もう あきらめましょう。
Moo akiramemashoo.

▶ もうすぐです。
Moosugu-desu.

▶ もう 出かけます。
Moo dekakemasu.

▶ もう 寝る 時間です。
Moo neru jikan-desu.

▶ もう 食事の 時間です。
Moo shokuji-no jikan-desu.

▶ もう 出発の 時間です。
Moo shuppatsu-no jikan-desu.

▶ もう 集合の 時間です。
Moo shuugoo-no jikan-desu.

▶ もう 始まっています。
Moo hajimatte-imasu.

60 a little more/ etc.

Requests ••••••••••••••••••••••••••••••••••••••

☐ May I have some more, please?

☐ Wait a little longer, please.

☐ Please hurry up.

☐ Please be quiet.

☐ Please speak a little more slowly.

☐ Please have some more. (*for food*)

Asking for a different item •••••••••••••••••••••••

☐ Don't you have a larger one?

☐ Don't you have a smaller one?

☐ Don't you have a cheaper one?

☐ Don't you have a plainer one?

☐ Don't you have a louder one?

Asking for permission •••••••••••••••••••••••••••••

☐ May I have a little more, please?

☐ May I stay here a little longer?

☐ May I keep it a little longer?

☐ May I wait here a little longer?

もうすこし　Moo sukoshi

▶もう すこし ください。
Moo sukoshi kudasai.

▶もう すこし お待ちください。
Moo sukoshi omachi-kudasai.

▶もう すこし 急いでください。
Moo sukoshi isoide-kudasai.

▶もう すこし 静かに してください。
Moo sukoshi shizuka-ni shite-kudasai.

▶もう すこし ゆっくり 話してください。
Moo sukoshi yukkuri hanashite-kudasai.

▶もう すこし おあがりください。
Moo sukoshi oagari-kudasai.

▶もう すこし 大きいのは ありませんか。
Moo sukoshi ookii-no-wa arimasen-ka.

▶もう すこし 小さいのは ありませんか。
Moo sukoshi chiisai-no-wa arimasen-ka.

▶もう すこし 安いのは ありませんか。
Moo sukoshi yasui-no-wa arimasen-ka.

▶もう すこし 地味なのは ありませんか。
Moo sukoshi jimi-na-no-wa arimasen-ka.

▶もう すこし 派手なのは ありませんか。
Moo sukoshi hade-na-no-wa arimasen-ka.

▶もう すこし いただいても いいですか。
Moo sukoshi itadaite-mo ii-desu-ka.

▶もう すこし いても いいですか。
Moo sukoshi ite-mo ii-desu-ka.

▶もう すこし お借りしても いいですか。
Moo sukoshi okari-shite-mo ii-desu-ka.

▶もう すこし お待ちしても いいですか。
Moo sukoshi omachi-shite-mo ii-desu-ka.

61 I have ~.

- [ ] I have my passport.

- [ ] I have my I.D. card.

- [ ] I have a suitcase.

- [ ] I have some luggage.

- [ ] I have a camera.

- [ ] I have a radio.

- [ ] I have a tape recorder.

- [ ] I have two cars.

- [ ] I have a country house.

- [ ] I have a VCR.

- [ ] I have traveler's checks.

- [ ] I have my credit card.

- [ ] I have a receipt.

- [ ] I have some small change.

- [ ] I have some coupons.

- [ ] I have a letter of introduction.

持っています　Motte-imasu

▶ パスポートを 持っています。
Pasupooto-o motte-imasu.

▶ 身分証明書を 持っています。
Mibunshoomeesho-o motte-imasu.

▶ スーツケースを 持っています。
Suutsukeesu-o motte-imasu.

▶ 荷物を 持っています。
Nimotsu-o motte-imasu.

▶ カメラを 持っています。
Kamera-o motte-imasu.

▶ ラジオを 持っています。
Rajio-o motte-imasu.

▶ テープレコーダーを 持っています。
Teepurekoodaa-o motte-imasu.

▶ 車を 2台 持っています。
Kuruma-o ni-dai motte-imasu.

▶ 別荘を 持っています。
Bessoo-o motte-imasu.

▶ ビデオデッキを 持っています。
Bideodekki-o motte-imasu.

▶ トラベラーズチェックを 持っています。
Toraberaazu-chekku-o motte-imasu.

▶ クレジットカードを 持っています。
Kurejittokaado-o motte-imasu.

▶ 領収証を 持っています。
Ryooshuusho-o motte-imasu.

▶ 小銭を 持っています。
Kozeni-o motte-imasu.

▶ クーポン券を 持っています。
Kuuponken-o motte-imasu.

▶ 紹介状を 持っています。
Shookaijoo-o motte-imasu.

62 I don't ~.

Hobbies ••

☐ I don't play any sports.

☐ I don't play golf.

☐ I don't ski.

☐ I don't skate.

☐ I don't bowl.

☐ I don't climb mountains.

☐ I don't fish.

☐ I don't like karaoke.

☐ I don't play the horses.

☐ I don't play mahjong.

When talking about sports and hobbies, we use the verb *Yarimasu* (Do). The sentences above are all negative, so let us look at some affirmative sentences: *Kazoku-de tenisu-o yarimasu* (The family plays tennis together); *Kon'ya booringu-o yarimasen-ka* (Would you like to go bowling tonight?); *Goshumi-wa nan-desu-ka* (What are your hobbies?)—*Shodoo-o yatte-imasu* (I practice calligraphy). Note also that you can talk about certain ↗

やりません Yarimasen

• •

▶スポーツは やりません。
Supootsu-wa yarimasen.

▶ゴルフは やりません。
Gorufu-wa yarimasen.

▶スキーは やりません。
Sukii-wa yarimasen.

▶スケートは やりません。
Sukeeto-wa yarimasen.

▶ボーリングは やりません。
Booringu-wa yarimasen.

▶登山は やりません。
Tozan-wa yarimasen.

▶釣りは やりません。
Tsuri-wa yarimasen.

▶カラオケは やりません。
Karaoke-wa yarimasen.

▶競馬は やりません。
Keeba-wa yarimasen.

▶麻雀は やりません。
Maajan-wa yarimasen.

habits or preferences with *yarimasu*: *Sake-mo tabako-mo yarimasen* (I don't drink and smoke).

When someone is asked **Yamada-san-wa gorufu-o nasaimasu-ka** (Do you play golf, Yamada-san?), he can answer yes by saying either *Hai, yarimasu* or *Hai, shimasu.* Both mean "Yes, I do." For women, though, **yarimasu** sounds just a little rough, and so there is a tendency to choose *shimasu*. ■

Index 1/Phrases

154

Index 2/Situations

Glossary

About the Authors :

Katsuaki Togo, a graduate of Waseda University's School of Education, is currently a professor of applied linguistics at Waseda. He has been active in many aspects of language teaching. For thirteen years he was the presenter of NHK's English Conversation program. He is also the author of many books on English language teaching and learning, including *Columbus English Course*, the junior high school textbooks published by Mitsumura Book Publishing Company, Ltd., and *Swift and Sure English Conversation*, published by The Japan Times.

Fujiko Motohashi is a graduate of Keio University's Department of Literature, and received her M. A. in Japanese language and literature education at Waseda University. For fifteen years she has been involved in teaching Japanese to foreigners and in instructing teachers of Japanese. She is currently teaching at the Tsuda Center for Japanese Language Teaching. She is a coauthor of *24 Tasks for Basic Modern Japanese, Vols. 1 & 2*, published by The Japan Times.